BAD GIRLS

BAD GIRLS

THE MEDIA, SEX AND FEMINISM
IN THE '90s

CATHARINE LUMBY

ALLEN & UNWIN

For Andrew Charker

First published in 1997 by
Allen & Unwin Pty Ltd
9 Atchison Street, St Leonards, NSW 2065 Australia
Phone: (61 2) 9901 4088
Fax: (61 2) 9906 2218
E-mail: frontdesk@allen-unwin.com.au
URL: http://www.allen-unwin.com.au

National Library of Australia
Cataloguing-in-Publication entry:

Lumby, Catharine.
    Bad girls: TV, sex and feminism in the '90s.

    Bibliography.
    Includes index.
    ISBN 1 86448 076 9.

    1. Women in mass media. 2. Sexism in mass media. 3.
    Feminism. I. Title.

305.42

Set in 10.5/13pt Garamond by DOCUPRO, Sydney
Printed by Australian Print Group, Maryborough, Vic.

10 9 8 7 6 5 4 3 2 1

Contents

'Whatever one thinks about woman,
feminism, at least is never One.'

Meaghan Morris, *The Pirate's Fiancée*

Acknowledgements

A number of people have encouraged me to keep writing over the years. Without them I'd be a wealthy lawyer. Thanks, in chronological order, to David Messer, Meaghan Morris, Alan Cholodenko, Robert Whitehead, Jenna Price, Mike Steketee, Max Suich, Pilita Clark, John O'Neill, Richard Glover, Frank Moorhouse, Robert Hughes and Toby Miller. John Hartley and Meaghan Morris deserve special mention here for their generous professional support and because their witty and prescient books were an important source of information for this one.

Benjamin David, Linda David, Moira Gatens and Elizabeth Jacka have all read significant parts of this book and the best of it owes a great deal to their insights.

A number of institutions and people attached to them have also been important sources of professional and personal support: Ashley Crawford, publisher of *Tension*, *21C* and *World Art*; Josephine Tiddy, South Australian Equal Opportunity Commissioner; Professor Philip Bell, Head of Mass Communications at Macquarie University; Keith Kirby and Robert Kostrewa at the Commonwealth Fund of New York; Chris Nash and Wendy Bacon at the University of

Technology; John Alexander and John Lyons at the *Sydney Morning Herald*; and Sophie Cunningham, my publisher at Allen & Unwin, who commissioned this book.

Rebecca Huntley and Emile Sherman both generously allowed me to quote from their unpublished research.

I'm grateful to Gregory Harvey and Shelly Cox for help with the book's design.

For lessons in questionable manners, from eating sweets in church to trashing bars, I have my girlfriends to thank, from the original Ravenswood gang—Laura Williams, Penny Galwey, Kyrsty Hannaford and Katrina Greenwood—to the more recently acquired but equally badly behaved—Pam Hansford, Louise Katz, Margo Kingston, Susan Kriete, Lisa McGregor and Julia Robinson.

This book would not have been written without the support of my family: Athol, Judy, Alison and Caroline Lumby.

And as someone who needs thanking in every category above, McKenzie Wark gets this final, grateful paragraph all to himself.

Introduction

In 1992, the *Australian* newspaper sent me to Melbourne to write an opinion piece about a conference on sex, women and the media. Before the conference, I took the opportunity to interview one of the key speakers, Dr Jocelynne Scutt, a prominent Australian feminist barrister and an opponent of degrading images of women in the media. Dr Scutt has spoken and written so frequently on the subject of sexism in the media she is often invoked as an expert on the media *by* the media. So it came as something of a shock to learn she didn't own a television set.

'You can't isolate yourself from the sexism that comes through every day on your television screen', she told me. 'I mean I do to a certain extent because I don't have television . . .'

When I recorded her comment in an essay published the following week in the *Australian* and went on to question her knowledge of contemporary television, she replied with an angry letter to the editor. 'I am', she wrote, '(to my sometime chagrin) "television literate"', because 'all those occasions I spend time in hotels and motels (a not inconsiderable part of my life) I switch on immediately I walk into the room, and switch off after watching to the early hours of the morning'.

Re-reading her letter now, Dr Scutt's peripatetic viewing habits strike me as more interesting than her refusal to have television in her house. Hotel rooms, after all, are traditional havens for lapses from domestic standards. The minibar, the in-room dining menu and the movie channel call the most virtuous interstate traveller from their laptop. Even for a critic burdened with the most exacting standards, watching television can't be all hard work in this kind of environment.

Ironically, Dr Scutt's relegation of television viewing to the chance hotel encounter is in perfect accord with the view of mass-media culture championed by a good number of the conservative and largely male academic establishment. Television watching is a guilty secret—something to be engaged in sparingly and in private.

FEMINISM AND THE PUBLIC SPHERE

When United States Republican Senator Bob Dole or Australian media critic Stuart Littlemore attack popular culture or 'trash' television it makes sense. Both men have apprehended a sea change in culture, a shift away from sober, rational and analytic debate and a widespread tendency in the media to focus on the private and the personal at the expense of larger public policy issues. Despite their political differences, both men have a real interest in preserving the traditional structure of the public sphere, which is founded on separating the domain of work, law, and public policy from the private world of the family, children, morality and intimate relationships. Like the thousands of other academics, journalists, politicians, judges and religious leaders who have denounced the tabloid media and Hollywood films for corrupting society and weakening democracy, they are defending a status quo which has served them well. But if we unpack the origins of the public sphere we can begin to see that its scope and structure haven't served all groups in society equally well. And from there, we can begin to question whether the tabloidisation of the media is really as bad for all members of society as many older male opinion makers suggest.

The English word for 'public' is derived from the Latin word for adult male, *pubes*. As John Hartley argues in his remarkable and, for a feminist reader, very useful book, *The Politics of Pictures*, the traditional Western notion of the public sphere is deeply rooted in this exclusivity—in the Greek agora and the Roman forum where adult free men could meet to vote, adjudicate disputes and discuss philosophy, the arts and the business of civic life, out of the reach of women, slaves and foreigners (Hartley 1992).

These ideals of open, rational and critical debate among free, educated equals have been central to traditional ideas about the media's proper role in the public sphere and, by extension, democracy. In this civilised scenario, journalism has a paternalistic, educative function—the media is simultaneously a canny watchdog of other public-sphere institutions and a mouthpiece for higher thought. There is a clear delineation between facts and opinions. No-one gets unduly carried away or emotional. Reporters disseminate objective, factual information, while seasoned, reasonable columnists smooth the sleeves of their corduroy jackets, sip their

Chardonnay and comment. The masses (always easily swayed and in need of guidance) presumably shut up and listen.

Somewhere along the patriarchal line though, something went terribly wrong with this picture. The media, as I will argue in this book, turned out to be a Trojan Horse. Newspapers, radio and television offered more than a window onto elite institutions like parliament, the courts, the professions and the business world—they offered the average citizen a point of view. With a point of view, came inevitable criticisms of the way the public sphere is run and demands that women and other minority groups have a part in doing the running. Suddenly, the barbarians weren't simply at the gates—they were inside, redecorating the castle in garish new colours.

Of course, those who've traditionally benefited from an exclusive public sphere aren't terribly impressed with the new, noisy shape of the agora. Understandably, they're keen to return to a world where the public and private spheres are clearly separated, where it's easy to tell high culture and low culture apart and where an 'expert' elite are the only people expected to have opinions.

Women, on the other hand, have very little to gain from a return to the good old days, since they were never welcome in the 'public' sphere in the first place. If anything, women might be expected to encourage cracks in the structure of the traditional public sphere. Yet, the opposite has been true. In the past decade, feminists have publicly joined forces with conservative critics of the media and popular culture. They have campaigned against 'sexist' ads and denounced violent and sexual content in books, films, magazines, music videos and video games. They have called for government inquiries into the potentially corrupting effects of new media technologies. They have lobbied for new forms of censorship for virtually every kind of popular medium. And they have done it with great success.

Susan Faludi's *Backlash: The Undeclared War Against Women* and Naomi Woolf's *The Beauty Myth*—both enormously popular works in Australia and the United States—exemplify the media bashing which dominates feminist debate in the 1990s. Elaborating her now famous Backlash theory, Faludi goes on a selective trawl through the mass media to find evidence of an 'undeclared war against women' and a 'bulletin of despair' posted everywhere for women to read and learn from (Faludi 1991). While distancing herself from a direct conspiracy-theory view of its role—'The press didn't set out with this, or any other intention; like any large institution, its movements aren't premeditated or programmatic'—she is all too ready to see the forces of conservatism pulling its strings, rendering it 'grossly susceptible to the prevailing political currents' (Faludi 1991, p. 101). Given her sketchy theory of how the media operates, it's not surprising that Faludi is also quick to place consumers in the 'dupe' basket. The entire public, she assumes, is simply swept along in the wake of the latest media fad (everyone, that is, except feminists like herself who have miraculously found some dry and high moral ground from which to survey the resultant flood).

Naomi Woolf is equally vague in her construction of The Beauty Myth—which, like The Backlash, turns out to be an amorphous form of mind control purveyed by the mass media. 'There is no legitimate historical or biological justification for the beauty myth', she writes. 'What it is doing to women today is a result of nothing more exalted than the need of today's power structure, economy, and culture to mount a counteroffensive against women' (Woolf 1991, p. 13). The evasive slippages between the terms 'myth', 'women', 'power structure', 'economy' and 'culture' are telling. Like Faludi, Woolf works by juxtaposing generalisations—and, in doing so, conveniently avoids the rather more complex task of addressing the relationships between media content, format and the viewing or reading context, which even the most basic account of the media demands.

Feminist campaigns against 'sexist' advertisements have begun to look equally simplistic. Knee-jerk claims that an image is 'sexist' are rarely backed up with coherent arguments. Prominent feminist politicians and public figures seeking broadcast air time routinely get away with vague assertions that an ad or a program purveys 'negative' or 'degrading' images of women—partly because the media itself has become so quick to give feminists the moral high ground. Yet, many of the claims feminists make about supposedly sexist images simply don't stack up. And placed in the context of the longstanding debate *within* the feminist community about these issues, they look contradictory and downright ill-conceived. Indeed, many of these supposedly feminist campaigns buy into the very cultural constructions of femininity feminists have railed against, such as the sanctity of women's bodies, the purity of motherhood and the taboo against showing women as sexual beings in their own right.

This contradiction arises because the pro-censorship feminist lobby fails to consider the ads they're complaining about in a broader context—to acknowledge, for instance, that all ads use images or concepts in a one-dimensional way—that, in the world of the thirty-second commercial spot, advertisers are keen to reduce all of us to a single desire or fear (despite the fact that the reception of an image is never so one-dimensional).

Even more alarmingly, when it comes to actual pornography, the pro-censorship feminist camp has long since abandoned debate with other feminists in favour of a pact with the kind of social conservatives who want to abolish abortion, criminalise homosexuality and dismantle feminism. Antiporn feminists have protested long and loud that they want nothing to do with traditional paternalistic notions of censorship. Yet, across Australia and the United States, they have knowingly formed alliances with 'family values' fundamentalists for the sole purpose of persuading the state to crack down on sexually explicit material. Under the antipornography banner, campaigns have been launched against everything from non-violent X-rated films (which many women consume) through lesbian erotica to pamphlets on sexually transmitted diseases. In the past three years, the explosive growth of the internet has provided pro-censorship feminists with a new target. In 1996, the United States Congress legislated to severely restrict the availability of sexually explicit material in cyberspace with the active support of prominent feminists.

Many of these campaigns for censorship, which are being waged in the name of feminism, are feminist campaigns in name only. Sections of the women's movement are actively ceding the legitimacy that feminism offers to powers that do not always have women's best interests at heart. And this raises the very real danger that the feminist legacy will be squandered on deals with conservative morals campaigners.

THE POLITICS OF FEMINIST POWER

For feminists who believe the women's movement should be focused on *producing* speaking positions for women, this extraordinary concern with *suppressing* speech is more than disturbing—it's a betrayal of feminist ideals.

In the past few years, feminists who feel alienated by the conservative face of popular feminism have begun speaking out. Katie Roiphe led the pack in 1993 with the publication of *The Morning After: Sex, Fear and Feminism on Campus*, a book attacking the 'zookeeper school' of feminism which treated men like beasts and women as victims. A host of authors have followed suit, including Christina Hoff Sommers' *Who Stole Feminism?*, Nadine Strossen's *Defending Pornography: Free Speech, Sex and the Fight for Women's Rights*, Rene Denfeld's *The New Victorians*, Beatrice Faust's *Backlash? Balderdash: Where Feminism Is Going Right*, Helen Garner's *The First Stone* and Kate Fillion's *Lip Service: the Truth about Women's Darker Side in Love*.

Although they are sometimes lumped together as 'postfeminist' or even 'antifeminist', the works listed above are highly diverse. There isn't space to examine the position of all of these authors in detail here, but I do want to briefly consider one book, because it exemplifies a position commonly attributed to the latest wave of feminists and it's one I want to explicitly distinguish myself from.

In *The New Victorians*, Rene Denfeld outlines her theory of where and why feminism has gone wrong. Citing widespread anti-male rhetoric, the antipornography movement and the lesbian separatist movement as evidence, Denfeld discerns a new Victorianism in contemporary feminism. She argues that, 'Today's feminists have created an overarching theory that blames male sexuality for the world's woes. In short, they believe that heterosexual intercourse—as an inherently invasive and oppressive act—is the root cause of all oppression' (Denfeld 1995, p. 11). This underlying theory, she writes, mimics the Victorian view of female sexuality—women as helpless victims who need to be protected from the brute reality of a male world. Young women, Denfeld concludes, have been turned off by the extremist elements who captured the feminist debate in the eighties, and are no longer prepared to call themselves feminists.

Unfortunately, Denfeld has succumbed to a number of overarching theories herself. For one thing, she treats both 'academic' and 'lesbian' feminists as complacent herds. Yet, key sections of both these groups have been instrumental in critiquing precisely the attitudes Denfeld complains about. Secondly, her theory about the resemblance of contemporary pro-censorship feminists to Victorian social purity campaigners is based on a simple and ultimately unhelpful opposition between the sexually liberated and the sexually repressed. Antiporn feminists quite rightly object to being dismissed as 'uptight' or 'puritanical'. Their opposition to sexually explicit material may *seem* like simple wowserism, but the philosophy behind it is a good deal more complex than mere abhorrence of sex.

It's ultimately unhelpful to dismiss pro-censorship feminists as 'new Victorians' or 'wowsers'. To do so ignores the historical volatility of the censorship debate and the diversity of ideas which have fuelled it. It reduces all opposition to pornography to the level of individual sexual 'enlightenment'.

Denfeld also positions her book as a generational salvo. Its subtitle is 'A Young Woman's Challenge to the Old Feminist Order'. The author turns up on the cover looking appropriately young, attractive and defiant—the reader is told in the author blurb that she 'trains as an amateur boxer'. The enticing sound of sharp generational sword play is all good box-office stuff, but any scrutiny of contemporary feminist debate shows that issues don't unpack neatly along generational or even political lines. It's messier than that.

While it's certainly tempting to reduce the current crisis to an opposition between a modern, enlightened feminist position and a naive, intellectually crude or old-fashioned one, I'm seeking a broader context in which to unpack contemporary debates about the extent to which media images and information are inherently harmful to women or discriminate against them. I am less interested in what pornography is (or isn't) or in what it does to people than in why feminists have become so interested in those questions. To put it simply I want to know what censorship and feminism have in common.

One of my key assumptions is that objects of knowledge like pornography aren't simply given. They're actively produced by the very people and institutions who investigate them. Politicians, the common law, feminists, psychiatrists, literary critics and religious belief systems are all, in one sense, manufacturers of pornography. And all to some extent want to reorganise the boundaries between acceptable erotica and pornography to legitimate their own ideological agenda.

The idea that pro-censorship feminists help 'produce' pornography may sound odd at first. But it's actually very important to my analysis of the relationship between bodies of knowledge such as feminism and the objects they critique. The idea that pornography is manufactured by groups who oppose it is grounded in French philosopher Michel Foucault's argument that sexuality is actively produced by forms of professional knowledge and institutions dedicated to speaking its truth—from the confessional box, to the psychiatrist's couch to talk shows. Foucault is interested in the way sexuality has come to be seen as a fixed aspect of our identity—as something, in other words, which tells us the truth about who we are. The twentieth century has been marked by a belief that we need to understand ourselves, even our unconscious selves, and that one of the keys is understanding our sexual identity.

Foucault turns this belief system on its head. Human sexuality, he argues, is not producing knowledge or truth, knowledge (the idea that we need to get to the truth) is producing sexuality. Disciplines and institutions which investigate sex—even the most scientific—are also a means of obtaining sexual pleasure, just as pleasure in sex is tied to trying to unravel its mystery (Foucault 1979).

Christian confession is intimately linked to the emergence of pornography itself. The rules of the confessional box—the requirement that the confessor catalogue and examine each unworthy sexual act and thought—is a powerful tool for teaching the connection between knowledge of sex and erotic pleasure. Pornography, in this light, doesn't arise because sex has been repressed, but because of the demand that we speak about it.

The idea that institutions (like the church or the law) and ideas or types of knowledge (like feminism or liberalism) produce the objects they claim to study or critique has implications which go beyond the censorship debate. It suggests we need to ask what kind of investment feminism has at any given time in the objects, institutions or practices it opposes or debates. Feminists have often observed that pornography is designed to give pleasure and a sense of power to an implicitly male viewer. But it's equally important to ask what kind of power and pleasure pro-censorship feminism derives from attacking pornography.

To come at this problem from another direction, I'm arguing that feminism needs to be conscious of its own power. Too often, feminists present themselves and their ideas as existing outside the power loop. That might have been appropriate in the days when women didn't have the vote and couldn't dispose of property in their own name, but it isn't helpful in an era when feminism has made some important inroads into government institutions, public policy and popular debate. In other words, feminists can't continue to argue that they're outsiders to state power, while designing legislation to promote their agenda. There's more at stake here than credibility. The broader point implicit in Foucault's argument is that if feminism is creeping into state power, then it's a fair bet state power is creeping into feminism. Perhaps in some ways and on some issues it should be. But not without a free and frank debate on what kind of relationship feminism ought to have to existing forms of power, in particular, repressive power like the power to censor. I explore the institutionalisation of feminism and its use of state power further in chapter eight.

Like the objects it's designed to contain, censorship is a highly contentious business. There are people who think that sex, sexual feelings and the proper representation of both are private matters. And there are those who think they need extensive public supervision by courts, police, parliaments and priests.

There's one thing, though, on which many people across the censorship spectrum agree: our sexual desires and behaviours tell us the truth about who we are. In contrast, throughout this book I remain sceptical of any claim that our sexual desires, fantasies or behaviours can offer us an insight into who we *really* are, regardless of whether the argument is mounted from a liberal, libertarian, feminist, religious, psychiatric or latex-loving perspective. Censorship is not a weapon (to oppress natural desires and sexualities) or a necessary evil (to protect the innocent and virtuous from the wanton) but a tool, whose shape and purpose changes according to who's wielding it. Nor is censorship simply a set of laws, regulations or procedures used to police images and information—it affects the meaning we give those images and information.

Feminism has an intense interest in the way women are represented. A great deal of that focus has devolved onto images which implicitly and explicitly sexualise women. The main thrust of the feminist attack on media images of women has been the claim that they reduce women to sexual objects designed to gratify male desires. The resulting discrimination against women is said to be so abhorrent—given that it supposedly involves stripping them of their humanity—that it overwhelms the harm caused by any diminution of the right to freedom of expression. It's hardly surprising that feminists who believe pornography puts women's lives at stake are unwilling to listen to free speech advocates.

As a result, over the past decade, pro-censorship feminists have sought to shift terms of the debate away from the freedom of speech issues, which have characterised obscenity law, and regroup them under the rubric of discrimination. In this framework, pornography and other allegedly sexist depictions of women are seen as harmful because they reduce women to their usefulness (generally sexual) to men.

Pro-censorship feminists also argue that the concept of free speech is itself a mask for discrimination—that free speech is, in real terms, the right of men to speak *at the expense of* women. For these reasons, pro-censorship feminists often object to being described as pro-censorship. Nonetheless, I've chosen to use the term 'pro-censorship' throughout this book because I believe there are major limitations to the pornography-as-discrimination argument (which I outline at length in chapter five) and because I think censorship describes the result of feminist campaigns against the media.

THE MEDIA AS VIRUS

In the past twenty-five years, feminists have spent a lot of time and intellectual and emotional energy analysing the way feminist values and concerns about the representation of women and gender politics have shaped and influenced the mass media. But they've spent very little time looking at how the mass media has shaped and influenced feminism.

As the term 'mass media' implies, the media is often talked about as an amorphous lump. Television, radio, videos, newspapers, alternative 'zines, Hollywood cinema, billboards, web sites, video games all get dumped in a box marked popular culture. Still images, text, film, computer graphics and email are frequently discussed as if they were all the same thing. Yet, few people would try the same thing with a Jane Austen novel and a Jackson Pollock canvas.

The 'mass' in media refers to audience reach rather than inherent homogeneity, and the way we receive and process any image or piece of information is bound up with the format and context in which we receive it. It's a point Marshall McLuhan made about the media when he said: 'The medium is the message'. Or, to quote a line about the media from David Cronenberg's film *Videodrome*—'It bites'.

The idea that the media is a monolithic institution which somehow speaks in the voice of mainstream patriarchy (with a capitalist accent) is ultimately unhelpful for understanding the relationship between feminism and the vertiginous spiral of images and information which defines contemporary culture. To use an old postmodern metaphor, the media is like a virus. It infects everything it touches, but it is also, in turn, changed by what it comes into contact with—it mutates.

Feminists have failed to grasp the contradictory, constantly shifting nature of contemporary mass-media imagery and to realise that the mass media is not a stable platform for pushing political or moral values of any single persuasion. The average nuclear family in contemporary sitcoms is now portrayed as a dysfunctional joke. Certainly some ads, programs and films present women as helpless victims and men as patriarchal heroes—but just as often these stereotypes are sent up. Consider the self-mocking macho stance Arnold

Schwarzenegger adopts in his action movies or the self-conscious sex goddess posturing of Madonna. The sheer proliferation of images has eroded the moral authority of any one social order—patriarchal or otherwise. It's this very collapse which has fuelled social revolutions such as feminism. Far from representing the voice of patriarchal authority, the mass media is a daily reminder of the unstable ground on which notions of gender, sexuality and even nationhood are built in the late twentieth century.

While I was writing this book, I bought a baseball cap which reads: Bitch. I found it in a Greenwich Village store which mostly caters to gay men. It's clearly meant to be worn with a camp attitude. I liked it for slightly different reasons—'bitch' is a traditional term for dampening the aspirations of uppity women and I figured it was time for a little reappropriation. But when I was buying groceries at my local store I was struck by a third potential reading. An African-American woman was staring at my cap with obvious horror—bitch connotes male sexual ownership in the black community. My baseball cap is a reminder of the way meaning changes with context, of the plurality of meanings which any image or phrase can carry, and of the tendency people have to reinvent and appropriate meaning for their own ends.

Throughout this book I take issue with feminist readings of media images and offer alternative accounts. I begin chapter one, for instance by describing an erotic encounter between two lovers, and a book and a watch, based on a Helmut Newton photograph. Like all accounts of images, my description is largely an account of what I want to see. In arming myself for a disagreement with people who see only molestation, degradation and sexual violence towards women in the photograph, I've reinvented it in my favour. I've minimised details which suggest cruelty on the part of the shadowy male figure, and I've opted to see the woman's apparent indifference as a sign of her intellectual self-absorption. I've altered the image in line with my desires.

It doesn't follow, though, that I'm misrepresenting the image, or that I somehow got it 'wrong'. Like all viewers I've simply interacted with what I see—interpreted the image on the basis of what I know and what I want to know. By the same token, I don't believe that pro-censorship feminists have somehow misunderstood the truth behind the images they critique. At times I may suggest other readings or point out aspects of an image which have been ignored—but a basic assumption always grounds my arguments: there is no single, 'true' reading of any image or representation. There are only points of view.

Of course, not all points of view are given equal weight in a given society. Feminism has historically been concerned with the dominant nature of one point of view in the production and consumption of images: a male, patriarchal perspective. Yet, the popular feminist critique of the media has *itself* become a dominant point of view. It has become self-satisfied and lazy. It has failed to take account of changes in popular culture and the media more generally. It is out of touch with the way people consume images.

Ultimately, I am arguing, you can't begin to understand contemporary culture if you start from the belief you can recognise the 'truth' of a given image or you know better than the people who consume it. The meaning of an image doesn't reside inside it, but in its rapid circulation.

TAKING IT PERSONALLY

Feminism got me a long way before I eventually got it. For starters, it got me an orange plastic model of the Apollo 11 spaceship you could actually sit in while you perfected your moon-landing technique. It got me parents who refrained from explaining the reality of gender politics at NASA in 1968. And it got me into the odd fight with boys at the school bus stop.

By the time I queued up with hundreds of other female students to enrol in a university degree, it had also got me weirdly, if temporarily, convinced that my future happiness lay in a Chanel suit and a mission to save large corporations from legal embarrassment. (This particular delusion began to die some years later, when a major law firm asked me, in an interview, how many babies I planned to have.)

Feminism gave my generation of middle-class women— the older end of the Gen X-ers—a bunch of stuff most of us didn't even know we had. An expectation we would find a career and support ourselves. A relatively guilt-free response to sex and relationships. And a major attitude problem with older men who insisted on addressing us as 'lassie'.

As a teenager, I regarded feminism as some weird hobby women of my mother's era had, along with spinning, Splades and sincerity. My perspective only began to shift some time after I began studying feminist theory at university. My mother and her friends would probably like to think that my change of heart was a sign of my burgeoning social conscience, produced by a series of personal encounters with the patriarchal infrastructure. But actually the thing that got me to pay attention to feminism was the lifestyle accessories it sanctioned. In a period when the wearing of Che Guevara T-shirts and Akubra hats was still mandatory among Marxists, mid-eighties feminism endorsed the wearing of red lipstick *with* combat boots, not to mention a simultaneous interest in table dancing and Luce Irigaray.

As it turns up in a series of courses taught in university, feminism has always been something more than a set of methods and ideas. It's also a fundamental challenge to the belief that you can and should separate theory from everyday life. It problematises the very idea of disinterested knowledge—at the same time as it poses a series of challenging intellectual questions.

Some feminists, particularly those who haven't had much to do with academic feminism recently, are inclined to dismiss contemporary feminist theory as apolitical, superficial and out of touch with the essence of feminism. What they miss, I think, is one of the central insights of feminism—the thing, in fact, which drew me to feminism in the first place: that politics are not simply a matter of appearances, appearances are a matter of politics too.

The challenge feminist theory provides to the idea of disinterested or pure knowledge has influenced the structure of this book and the style it's written in. *Bad Girls* isn't organised according to linear logic. The chapters overlap and intersect like circles in a Venn diagram. The same themes and arguments crop up in relation to various topics—in fact, one of the aims of the book is to show how debates on issues like video-game violence, X-rated videos, tabloid television and the internet are related.

In general terms, this book deals with contemporary

feminist debates on the media and examines recent controversies. Chapters one and three through seven take up controversies which have flared up around issues like violence in the media, sexism in advertising, the demeaning content of tabloid media and feminist concerns about pornography on the internet, and offer an alternative feminist view. The second chapter is an exception. It looks at the history of censorship debates in Australia and the institutions and laws which have been used to regulate popular culture and the mass media. The final chapter offers a direct response to some of the concerns senior second wave feminists have expressed to a younger generation and looks at where feminism is going in the immediate future.

This book is, in many senses, a crossover book. Like the mass culture formats it analyses, it roams across traditional boundaries between academic theory, reportage and journalistic polemic. As such, it reflects my personal belief that cross-fertilisation between knowledges and institutions strengthens rather than weakens understanding.

The gap between audiences and different types of knowledge is not always the most comfortable place to be, but it's also a highly productive place from which to view the hybrid beast we call the media.

One: Beyond the real woman

A woman is sitting in a chair reading a book. She has showered and put on a satin nightgown ready for bed. Her lover, who has just arrived home late from a business appointment, comes up behind her and slips his hand inside the gown to fondle her breast. The gown falls off her shoulder. Aroused but keen to finish the last few sentences on the page before her, the woman begins touching herself through the clinging fabric while her eyes linger on the book.

It's a common enough portrait of sexual intimacy played out in different ways in millions of Australian homes daily. One partner expresses desire, the other savours the attention before reciprocating. The roles are easily reversed. A woman might bite her boyfriend's ear or kiss his neck to seduce him away from a late-night television show. She might slap her girlfriend's bare bottom with a hairbrush, for that matter. The game of seduction is open to both genders and all sexualities.

Yet, when a photograph by Helmut Newton depicting a scene similar to the one I just described was used to advertise a watch in a major Australian magazine, the Australian

Advertising Standards Council was inundated with complaints, and the advertiser, a Sydney jeweller, was forced to withdraw the ad. The complaints varied in tone and scope, but most made one essential point: the advertisement was sexist because the scene shown degraded and humiliated women. An act which many women would accept if it occurred in their own lounge room became misogynist when depicted in a photograph.

Leader of the Australian Democrats Cheryl Kernot added her clout to the swarm of complaints, denouncing the ad as 'derogatory and demeaning in the extreme' and 'blatantly insulting not just to women but also to men'. The outrage and horror provoked by the ad was summed up by the following complaint:

> It is the most offensive advertisement I have ever been subjected to. It conveys the dangerously misleading message that women condone and enjoy being molested by men and that this behaviour is completely normal. It objectifies women, demeans women and advocates sexual harassment and abuse, which is absolutely unacceptable. I am disgusted by this advertisement and feel that printing it is yet another crime against women . . .

In the 1990s, anybody who reads newspapers, watches television or listens to the radio will recognise this critique as feminist. Public concern about sexism in advertising and the mass media has exploded over the past decade. In 1995, one third of the ads most complained about to the Australian Advertising Standards Council drew complaints of sexism.

These complaints have been echoed by broader public campaigns in which senior politicians and members of the judiciary have joined established women's groups, such as the Women's Electoral Lobby (WEL), in denouncing particular ads. The media itself has routinely acknowledged these concerns in hundreds of news reports, feature articles, talkback shows and current affairs stories. Public interest in campaigns against sexist imagery is so keen that the chairman of the Australian Advertising Standards Council speculated that some advertising agents are even intentionally incorporating feminist-baiting imagery into their ads to cash in on the free publicity.

Speaking on behalf of the then federal government in her capacity as Minister Assisting the Prime Minister on the Status of Women, Labor Senator Rosemary Crowley summed up this widespread community concern about the representation of women in advertising and in the media. She said:

> For more than a decade, research has found that the portrayal of women in the media and in advertising is grossly insufficient and inappropriate . . . Where women are portrayed they are too often shown as unintelligent, or sexy, or as housewives responsible only for housework. As one woman told Consumer Contact research in 1992 'you are either a bimbo or a drone—a sex object or a drudge' . . . Too often women are depicted as sex objects or victims of sensationalised and often violent sex crimes. Sexist stereotyping of women persists in journalism and advertising (Crowley 1993).

Senator Crowley's speech relies on familiar phrases—'sex object', 'sexist stereotyping', 'inappropriate portrayal of women' —to bolster a feminist critique of the media. But what do these terms really mean? Is a sexist or demeaning image something universal which anyone with the right feminist consciousness can spot? Or are these terms subjective? Are all feminists agreed on what these terms mean? And exactly to whom and for whom is Senator Crowley speaking? In this chapter I want to examine some of these questions by looking at the arguments directed at the Sydney

4

jeweller's ad and teasing out their origins in academic and popular debates.

FROM NAKED TO NUDE AND BACK AGAIN

It is a most offensive advertisement having connotations of women as objects, property and entirely at the disposal of men (complaint about the jeweller's ad).

From Praxiteles' Aphrodite, whose form Pliny claimed drove one young man to indecently assault the statue, to feminist campaigns against lingerie ads, naked women have always caused trouble—a fact British art historian Kenneth Clark acknowledges in his infamous 1956 book *The Nude*. He wrote:

The desire to grasp and be united with another human body is so fundamental a part of our nature that our judgement of what is known as 'pure form' is inevitably influenced by it. One of the difficulties of the nude as a subject for art is that these instincts cannot lie hidden (Clark 1990, p. 8).

Clark admits the 'difficulties' of the nude, but he ultimately wants to separate the ideal form of the artistic nude from the messy realities of the naked body. In the first chapter of *The Nude*, Clark draws his famous distinction between being naked and nude. To be naked is to be deprived of clothes and in a state of shame; to be nude is to be a work of art. This schism between the naked body and the nude is a cherished premise in Western art history—

not least because it's legitimised an awful lot of babe watching under the guise of disinterested academic work.

Ultimately, Clark's 'universal' and 'natural' insights into beauty and art rest on a hidden gendered order. Referring to a Boucher nude, which depicts a fetching young beauty sprawled tummy-first on a couch, Clark writes: 'By art Boucher has enabled us to enjoy her with as little shame as she is enjoying herself' (Clark 1990, p. 149). The universal 'us' is, of course, a coded address to 'we men'.

The concealed gender politics of the nude in Western art is a cornerstone of popular feminist critiques of the representation of women in general. At its most basic, the feminist critique amounts to a simple reversal of Clark's terms—naked 'natural' bodies of real women are juxtaposed with false, idealised nudes designed by men to give pleasure to men. In his immensely popular 1972 book *Ways of Seeing*, John Berger summed up the argument this way:

> To be naked is to be oneself.
>
> To be nude is to be seen naked by others and yet not recognised for oneself. A naked body has to be seen as an object in order to become a nude . . . Nakedness reveals itself. Nudity is to be placed on display.
>
> To be naked is to be without disguise.
>
> To be on display is to have the surface of one's own skin, the hairs of one's own body, turned into a disguise . . . (Berger 1986, p. 54).

Comparing contemporary advertisements to fine-art nudes (with scant regard for the complex iconography of either), Berger argued that our essential way of seeing women hasn't changed over the centuries—the ideal spectator is always assumed to be male and images of women are designed to please and flatter him. But as a number of feminist art historians have subsequently pointed out, Berger's formula is as simplistic and ahistorical as Kenneth Clark's. All Berger does is swap Clark's terms about. He takes the nude off the pedestal and replaces it with the naked female body. Nature, in other words, takes over where Art left off.

In the mid-seventies, film theorist Laura Mulvey wrote a famous essay extending this debate about the fine-art nude to popular culture. Following an intellectual trend for rethinking culture using Freud's psychoanalytic theories of the unconscious and desire, Mulvey argued that conventional Hollywood narrative cinema is driven by 'the neurotic needs of the male ego'. As a result, female stars are presented almost solely as passive sexual objects for male viewers. Male stars, on the other hand, are 'real' characters who move the plot forward and provide men in the audience with a point of identification inside the narrative (Mulvey 1989, p. 26). Mulvey's argument is ultimately a lot more complex than Berger's. But she works with the same basic assumption that contemporary Western systems of representation are based around an active male spectator and a passive female figure.

A common feminist analysis of the Newton photo would point to the half-turned pose of the woman as evidence of her passivity. Like traditional fine-art nudes shown staring, self-absorbed, into mirrors, the woman in the satin gown enhances the male onlooker's voyeuristic pleasure in her body by demurely averting her gaze towards the book. The fact that the man is clothed, standing and anonymous (because we can't see his face) can also be read as evidence that the woman is a vulnerable object of desire, while the man is simply there as a surrogate pair of hands and eyes for the thousands of anonymous male viewers.

At first glance, it's all plausible enough—but so are hundreds of other interpretations. For one thing, the woman is reading a book—an activity she doesn't seem eager to hurl aside just because hubby's home from the office. For another, she's touching *herself*—behaviour which suggests there's a little more to their sexual relationship than penetration.

Reading images is never simple—whether we're talking watch ads or Titian's *Venus of Urbino*. In a culture saturated with reproduced images, it gets even more complex. For one thing, images don't stand alone—they constantly quote from other images, lending them a layered, half-seen dimension. For another, images don't stop at their own visual borders—they're affected by what frames them. How we read an image, in other words, depends largely on where we see it, when we see it, what preconceptions we bring to it and what we know about it in advance.

Which prompts the question: why insist on reading images like the Sydney jeweller's ad as demeaning to women? Why teach women to read images in a way that makes them feel bad about themselves? Why not encourage them to make creative readings of images and to appropriate and reinvent female stereotypes to their own advantage? Continually stressing the patriarchal reading of an image which can be read in other ways is hardly empowering for women. In fact, it's a strategy which cedes awesome power to images and to the people who produce them and which denies the ability women demonstrate daily to use imagination, critical resistance and humour in negotiating images and life in general.

SELLING SEX

It uses a woman's body to attract attention to a man's watch. There is obviously no connection between the two things and is therefore a blatant use of womanhood for advertising. And, as the last two sentences show, the woman has become an object comparable to a watch, available to give pleasure to the man (complaint about the jeweller's watch ad).

It has become an item of faith in popular feminist debate that it's wrong to use women's bodies to sell things. The equation is simple—in a capitalist and patriarchal society, women's use-value is reduced to their sexual usefulness to men. Like watches and widgets, women are packaged and commodified for the pleasure of the dominant sex. Lots of those who complained about the jeweller's watch ad picked up on the accompanying text as evidence of precisely this. It read: 'When you see this model in the flesh, you'll express your desire for it on sight. After all we never told you to look but not touch'.

Ironically, in this case the advertiser has also subjected Helmut Newton's photograph to a narrow interpretation. The copywriter has missed—or ignored—the ambiguities of desire lurking in the image which could be mobilised to attract consumers. And as if to compound this irony, by focusing attention on a reading of the image which renders the woman's body and the watch equivalent, the copywriter has encouraged an opposite and equally narrow interpretation by complainants. In both cases, the ambiguities of desire, images of desire and our desire for images is flattened out into a simplistic opposition that does no justice to the complexity of these issues.

Using the desire for female flesh to sell watches is hardly exceptional in a society which packages, advertises and sells everything from childbirth classes to funerals. Every day, all around us, our most intimate physical, emotional and intellectual desires are constantly invoked to sell almost anything. Advertisers play on our fears of baldness, impotence, weight gain, body odour, disease, desire for youth, success, and beauty.

The feminist campaign against purportedly sexist images of women in the mass media derives much of its rationale from a pseudo-Marxist critique of commodification. United States author Naomi Woolf used this critique as the cornerstone of her bestseller, *The Beauty Myth*. She argued:

> Since men have used women's 'beauty' as a form of currency in circulation among men, ideas about 'beauty' have evolved since the Industrial Revolution side by side with ideas about money, so that the two are virtual parallels in our consumer economy . . . women have learned to understand their own beauty as part of this economy (Woolf 1991).

It's an argument which was already well travelled when Woolf got her hands on it, and which flows from an ideological connection forged in the seventies, when the women's movement emerged from the broader leftist movement for social and political reform. Early Marxist feminists, such as Shulamith Firestone and Juliet Mitchell, argued that the liberal feminist obsession with legal inequalities and employment discrimination did not grasp the larger social and economic revolution needed to overthrow patriarchy. Today, however, the sharp divisions between the Marxist branch of feminism and liberal feminism have effectively dissolved in popular feminist debate. The commodification critique is now as common at a lawyer's dinner party as it is in a student newspaper.

But the popularity of this critique is no indication of serious reflection on the issue it purports to analyse. The crusade against 'sexist' images in the mass media remains riven with contradictions and unexamined assumptions which are often recycled without comment by younger feminists. The following excerpt from the 1993 manifesto of People Initiating Education Campaigns Eliminating Sexism (PIECES), published in the Macquarie University newspaper, *Arena*, is a classic instance of the simplistic parroting which can result:

P.I.E.C.E.S. are a group of groovy people who are sick of constantly being bombarded by demeaning, sexist, misogynist and harmful images of women and are actually doing something about it . . . It is not right that society, through its media images, has placed so many expectations on women to conform to the 'ideal' body size, which usually consists of Size 8, wafer-thin people who are starving themselves to reach this culturally (mass media) imposed definition of beauty. Control of women's bodies is taken away from the women and replaced with the notion that women are commodities, showpieces and objects which are used to sell products (PIECES 1993, p. 5)

In the PIECES manifesto, 'society' and 'the media' are big, hostile, abstract entities which exist 'over there'—as if PIECES were somehow able to stand outside the world the rest of us live in. PIECES' argument relies on the notion that 'the media' are hostile to all feminist critiques. Yet, the very argument PIECES is trying to make about the media has already gained widespread currency *in* the media. Which is exactly how PIECES wound up on television when the group protested in the lobby of the Consolidated Press building in Sydney. PIECES was, no doubt, trying to attract media attention, and the media were happy to oblige.

But let's take a closer look at the logic of PIECES' argument. Women, according to PIECES, are the victims of a powerful and apparently well-coordinated institution—the mass media—which has conspired to take away 'control' of their bodies. The 'dehumanising' aim of this campaign is to brainwash them into conforming to an 'ideal' body size, for the purpose of pleasing men and selling diet products. What this Orwellian vision of female victimhood, in which real women's bodies are misrepresented by media propaganda, ignores is the dynamic relationship between the media, capital and social identity. Separating real women's bodies from their fake media-endorsed clones is not that easy. To begin with, anyone who claims to be able to make the distinction between real women and false media images of them is claiming they're able to view things from outside the media-reality loop. But, as I argue throughout this book, everyday reality, and our perceptions of it, are continually filtered through the media's lens. We experience the majority of new phenomenon, people and events via television, the print media and radio. This mediated reality flows seamlessly in and out of our 'real' time experience of reality—we often refer to and debate news items as if we had experienced them first hand. Separating this flow of images and ideas— and its influence on our perceptions of everyday reality, other people and ourselves—is no simple matter. Secondly, if the media really *is* as influential as PIECES suggests, it's hard to see how they've escaped its manipulative power and found a vantage point to critique it from.

The bottom line is that PIECES, and many other more sophisticated feminists, are ultimately forced to argue they simply know better than the average woman—that they've discovered the 'truth'. But as the Marxist debate which originally spawned this notion of 'false' consciousness has recognised, it's a pretty patronising attitude for feminists to hold about 'other' women.

The 'reality' about the interaction between the mass media (in this case, advertising), women and identity in late capitalist society is far more complex than this oppositional model in which men are patriarchs, buyers and producers and women are reduced to victims, commodities and consumers.

SEXY OR SEXIST?

I find it blatantly sexual and sexist, and not the kind of thing one expects to find in one's morning paper (complaint about the Sydney jeweller's ad).

Addressing a conference, on sex and censorship, Australian Consolidated Press director and publisher Richard Walsh was hissed and occasionally shouted down as he attempted to deliver his paper. In popular feminist terms, Walsh is *the* enemy: a white, powerful male responsible for mass-media publications which include the Australian straight, single-girl's bible *Cleo* and the blue collar, satirical tits-and-bums magazine *Picture*. In his speech, Walsh addressed various criticisms of his publications, including claims that his women's publications assume their readers are only interested in pleasing men, while his men's publications please their readers with degrading images of women. Throughout his talk, he returned to one essential question: how are men (or in Walsh's words, 'smallish, sometimes bespectacled 51-year-old magazine publishers') supposed to reconcile the feminist demand that women be allowed to explore their own sexuality with the feminist campaign against sexually explicit or alluring images in the media?

The desire to drown out Walsh's straightforward question demonstrates how much it needles. Despite complaints that Walsh was failing to grasp the complexity of feminist debate, his query, in fact, identifies an important contradiction in the pro-censorship feminist camp. Female sexuality, the argument goes, has been denied and suppressed under patriarchy. Women have been treated as fundamentally alien creatures, as the fainting guardians of romance, home and hearth. They are blushing strangers to the bestial lust which springs from men's loins. At precisely the same time, however, many pro-censorship feminists argue that women *are* fundamentally different from men—that women's sexuality is somehow gentler and sweeter, and that objectification is a male sexual practice and good women don't do it. The second part of this argument reinforces some of the patriarchal notions feminists are complaining about in the first.

Pro-censorship feminists argue in response that they are not against sexually explicit images *per se*—just male-defined ones—and that women need to redefine sexual desire and their own sexuality outside the terms of the objectifying male gaze. Feminist Janice Raymond, for instance, envisions a sexuality 'rooted in lesbian imagination', which involves 'the presence of a whole human life', and which jettisons an objectifying, impersonal sexuality for one which includes 'the ability to touch and be touched' (Raymond 1993, p. 176).

It's a vision of sexuality, at least as Raymond articulates it, which amounts to a denial of the important role voyeurism and fantasy play in the lives of many men and women—straight and queer. Raymond, and other lesbian feminists who share her views, believe that sex as we know it is inextricably linked into the patriarchal structure of our society and that gender inequality is directly promoted by heterosexual behaviours, including voyeurism, flirtation and penetration.

But what would be left of sexual pleasure if Raymond's utopia came to pass? Is desire, or any kind of human interaction, possible without objectifying other people? And is equality a relevant goal in sexuality? Certainly, the opposition to Raymond's project is likely to be larger than a misogynist male cohort—plenty of hetero women, dykes, S/M practitioners and gay men are addicted to their daily dose of penetration too.

These complex questions about the relationship between sexuality and sexism are often effaced in public feminist debate, where sex is used as a shorthand for sexist. Complaints received by the Australian Advertising Standards Council consistently illustrate the crossover between objections to the sexual content of ads and objections to their sexism. Complaints about an Australian ad for Berlei bras captioned, 'We think more about what goes into your bra than your boyfriend', for example, attracted the following two complaints. The first criticised the billboard for implying that 'women's breasts are possibly the most important part of them' and for reinforcing the 'woman/body/object image'. The second complained that the ad 'encourages promiscuous thoughts and behaviour', undermines 'the God-given institution of marriage by suggesting that a "boyfriend" is akin to a husband', and 'degrades womanhood to the level of animal instinct'. Another complaint of sexism concerned an ad for *Cleo* magazine which illustrated a survey finding 'that 77 per cent of women prefer to make love in the dark' with a shot of a man and woman on a train that disappears briefly into a tunnel.

Clearly, some of this confusion between concerns about sexism and the portrayal of sexuality stems from the constant collision of complaints by social conservatives and feminist complaints. While this intersection certainly doesn't prove that all feminists are really wowsers in disguise, nor does it excuse feminists from confronting the ramifications of this crossover or the hybrid position it has opened up in public debate.

A complaint about a Nivea commercial which included a glimpse of a woman's breasts illustrates the ease with which feminist rhetoric is often grafted onto traditional conservative concerns:

I am writing to express my extreme disappointment with this new campaign. I do enjoy the actual ad, but do we need *nipples*? I have no hang up concerning the female body, but do we need to view them while watching a program that does not have sexual innuendos? Surely, the woman concerned could have worn a towel. Or does Nivea really stand for nipples . . . ? We have enough women in ads, 'selling' things to men.

The real nature of the complaint here is difficult to grasp. The complainant tries to defuse claims of puritanism by stating that he or she has 'no hang up', but then goes on to place a traditionally conservative priority on modesty. Confusingly, the complaint ends by invoking a feminist criticism—the woman's body is being used to 'sell things' to men.

Pro-censorship feminists are too quick to argue that any similarity between their own objections to an image and those of the religious fundamentalists is simply a case of mistaken identity. But the mushrooming alliances between pro-censorship feminists and social conservatives that I will analyse later in this book suggests pro-censorship feminist rhetoric has provided a cosy haven for the right. It would be both foolish and arrogant to suggest the benefits of this relationship only flow one way or that the fit is entirely coincidental.

Indeed, the objection that advertising turns women's bodies into commodities has clear echoes of traditional Christian morality which objects to anyone doing anything with a woman's body not prescribed by God, or by a narrowly defined notion of woman's essential nature—which amounts to the same thing.

Unwittingly, secular liberal feminist arguments now often

share a narrowly normative and limiting idea of what it means to be female with traditional Christian moralists. The tragedy is that feminism is becoming complicit with an ideology that wants to deny women the right to control their own bodies.

HOLY MOTHERS

My whole family find the concept of the photo utterly deplorable and completely unnecessary. It degrades women and is inappropriate for a *family* newspaper (complaint about the Sydney jeweller's ad).

In 1993, the Toyota company was forced to withdraw a print ad which showed the torso of a very pregnant woman cropped upwards from below the breasts captioned: 'There's nowhere more comfortable than inside a wide body'. Former Minister Assisting the Prime Minister on the Status of Women, Senator Margaret Reynolds shot off a press release urging Australian women to make complaints to Toyota dealers, the Advertising Standards Council and newspapers which ran the ad. Her concern? The image was 'insulting and dehumanising, firstly because it ridiculed pregnancy, and secondly because the picture showed a headless woman'. Senator Reynolds' complaint was routinely accepted as 'feminist' by reporters who picked up on her press release. It's a position, though, which arguably endorses as many traditional views of femininity as it attacks. The notion that maternity must be preserved from ridicule—that it is somehow sacred—is, after all, one that fundamentalist Christians and anti-abortion protestors are more than happy to endorse.

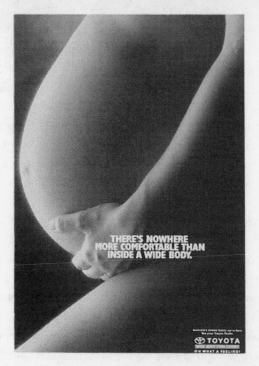

Marcus's birl "Loch Dawg"

What's more, Senator Reynolds' complaint that the woman is dehumanised by being shown headless is hard to accept given that this device arguably desexualises the woman by concealing her breasts.

At the end of the day, many of the supposedly feminist complaints about Australian ads amount to little more than an endorsement of the need to preserve women's bodies from profanation. The language of the protests says it all—the complaints cite 'disrespect', 'degradation' and the 'demeaning' of women's bodies. Yet what's at stake in the inverse? Exaggerated respect for women and the need to protect society from public displays of their bodies and their sexuality are, after all, trademark catchcries of religious and political groups that want to keep women confined to the domestic sphere.

A 1984 religious pamphlet circulated in Australia illustrates the point. Sexually arousing or erotic images of women, the anonymous writer argues, drag women down 'making them into things that people use', diminishes men, 'who are also diminished when the status of their sisters is diminished', and seriously damages children by teaching them that 'women are inferior and subservient; that sex is not a beautiful activity expressing affection, trust and love between man and woman'. Such images rob children 'of the proper sense of wonder at the mysterious process by which their own self came into being'. The pamphlet then urges recipients to protest to various MPs 'as a Christian, with love'. Amusingly it also suggests writing to the wives of the MPs, even though Susan Ryan, Ros Kelly, Anne Summers and Janet Strickland are four of the public officials named ('You Can Stop the Flood of Pornography' 1984).

In their defence, feminists who are concerned about sexist advertising are quick to point out that they aren't disturbed by the depiction of female sexuality—just by 'unrealistic' images of it. *Women and Media*, a booklet distributed by the federal government's National Working Party on the Portrayal of Women in the Media, puts the argument succinctly in its 'sexuality' section. Women, the booklet argues, 'resent the fact that the media often depicts them as thin, young and beautiful'. This is an image, that 'women—but not men—are pressured to emulate and which stems from societal expectations that women are objects of beauty, and which can in turn lead to illness'. Gratuitous display of female sexuality in magazines, the text concludes, 'has resulted in a public outcry from women' (Office of the Status of Women 1993b).

It's an argument which fails to address the central question it raises: exactly what do 'real' images of women's sexuality look like. To turn the problem around, sexuality may not be an area which is all that amenable to reality in the first place. If anything, it's a zone infused by the constant desire to reinvent ourselves and others. There's no doubt advertisers 'use' this aspect of sexuality to heighten our desire for products (the product, in effect, is being offered up *as* a substitute for the elusive object of desire). But it's one thing to acknowledge the möbius strip which runs between sex and capital, and quite another to argue that most women resent 'gratuitous' displays of sexuality in the media. What women tell market researchers, after all, and where they put their spending power may be two different things.

Commenting on the report, the chairperson of the Working Party, Anne Deveson, remarked that the media industry was ignoring women at its own peril and that 'media that reflects the diversity of women's lives reflects reality. It is good business. It succeeds' (Loane 1993, p. 8). It's a statement which raises the question of whether the public policy feminists who put the report together are really prepared to countenance such diversity. When they talk about 'reality' and 'diversity' are they happy to include everything from *Ms* magazine to X-rated videos? Or is 'reality' a code word for a preordained point of view?

WHAT DO REAL WOMEN WANT?

The battle over what ought to appeal to 'real' women was illustrated by a 1995 clash between a Sydney local council's anti-sexism committee and four young female advertisers. The council ordered the removal of a shampoo ad on a billboard over Sydney's Victoria Road which showed two sexy young women flaunting their muscular, partly clad bodies. But the writer, art director, photographer and client service manager, who were all women, argued that the ad constituted a legitimate appeal to the average young woman who was confident enough to be both independent and sexual.

The fact that women produced the ad does not guarantee that it's magically 'free' of patriarchal values—but it does suggest that 'real' women are a little more elusive and less docile than some feminist claims suggest. This concern with 'real' women can be traced back to the earliest feminist studies of the media which set out to show how media stereotypes of women reflected the desires and needs of men. In *Media She*, a book about media sexism published in 1974, Patricia Edgar and Hilary McPhee balanced stereotyped images of women with 'good' examples. They wrote:

> Over two months we read women's magazines, a range of daily newspapers and journals and came up with a mass of examples—all degrading or exploiting women—and half a dozen advertisements of 'real' women with real intelligences doing real tasks, and these from an American feminist magazine, *Ms* (Edgar & McPhee 1974, p. 2).

A decade later, Women's Electoral Lobby spokesperson on sexist advertising Diana Wyndham, was reiterating exactly the same concerns in an article entitled 'Advertisers' Woman, 80s Woman: Which Twin is the Phony?'. By this time the issue of sex stereotypes and the media had produced a voluminous literature and a complex debate, and some feminists were beginning to question the idea of censoring unwanted ads. In a 1981 article Helen Grace and Ann Stephen criticised the notion that personal and political change is a simple matter of 'peeling back the layers of conditioning to discover the real woman', and argued that the time had come to assess the usefulness of the 'sexist' tag in understanding media images of women (Grace & Stephen 1981, p. 15). Their article came at the start of an important trend away from a reactive and moralistic appraisal of the media in theoretical feminist work. Unfortunately, it's a trend which has had little impact on public policy debate on the subject. In 1993 the cover of a federal government brochure advising women on media still carried an image pointedly entitled 'Self Portrait with Honesty'.

From community media watchdog organisations like Mediaswitch to federal government reports on the portrayal of women in the media, the public debate on women and advertising is still dominated by a vision of culture in which 'good' feminist portrayals of women will eventually replace 'false' advertising images. At best, it's a self-serving and utopian view, at worst, it does the very thing feminists claim advertisers do: it patronises female consumers and ignores their needs.

The paradox is that when a handful of feminists start speaking on behalf of all 'women' and claiming to know what women want, they start sounding like the oppressive partriarchal advertisers they're attacking. The idea that media images need to be edited or critiqued by any group of experts—feminist or other—is an authoritarian one, which denies women the power to negotiate images on their own behalf. There are times when most of us wish someone would take away the burden of our desires and impose a consistent moral order on us—stop us watching *Melrose Place*, lusting after Chanel make-up, reading articles on Demi Moore or buying another book on feminist philosophy when we already own fifteen we haven't read. But if feminism is true to its own critique of patriarchy, feminists need to be extremely wary of claiming they know what's good for other women.

It's time for public policy feminists to jettison a position which simply exchanges 'bad' idealised women for 'good' real ones. It's also time to quit telling women what they want, and to start looking at what they buy. The latter involves a recognition that consumer behaviour is a lot more complex than the responses a group of women give to a survey designed by feminists. It involves a recognition of the role that desire, fantasy and guilt play in the way we consume media images. And, more importantly, it involves a recognition that there's no one 'real' woman feminists have been authorised to speak for.

In this sense, all feminists could arguably learn a lot from the contemporary advertising industry, which treats all of us like a series of schizophrenic fragments—multiple selves capable of assimilating and acting on totally contradictory desires and needs. In the world of advertising, women exist as an impossible chain of contradictory selves—as savvy urban professionals, as bleary-eyed exhausted mothers, as acid-tongued liberated lovers, as repentant guilty daughters, as babes, businesswomen and bitches. But how different is this reality from the 'reality' of everyday life in the late twentieth century?

Advertisers have been refining the question: what does the woman want for most of the twentieth century. And it's here, perhaps, that feminism ought to have more in common with advertising than some of its proponents think.

Precisely because its only goal is to make us buy more stuff, advertising often evinces more respect for the nuanced, complex and conflicted lives, loves and desires of women than some strands of feminism. And while the best advertising seduces us, feminism too often simply wants to prescribe what 'real' women ought to want. Rather than trying to regulate and control images of women in the name of some preordained norm, feminism ought to be encouraging a broad range of images of and for women, in the media and in everyday life.

A viable feminist approach to media images needs to recognise, develop and enhance women's abilities to negotiate images. Which surely must begin, not with a campaign to reinforce the idea that images are demeaning and degrading to women, but with a campaign to show what the diversity of women can, and regularly do, make of images and themselves.

Two: Feminists, censors and Australian sensibilities

They're corrupting our children, degrading our women, desensitising our society and fuelling a surge in violent crime. Only last week Sydney's major newspaper ran a front-page story linking the evil actions of a callous gunman to their influence. Church groups and women have launched a campaign to put a stop to this tidal wave of trash. A federal minister has taken note of the public outcry and promised to ban them.

The year? 1934. The problem? American comic books. Making a claim which is equally popular today, the Sydney *Sun* newspaper ran a front-page article on 1 July 1934 which blamed a 'brazen' hold-up on a robbery depicted in an American comic book. Politicians and community groups across the political spectrum were soon beating the censorship drum. The case against this dangerously influential filth was clear from a moral, patriotic, educational and protectionist point of view. The imported back copies were even literally dangerous to public health—after all, Americans fished them out of hospital garbage bins before dumping them on our shores. Within a few years, the scourge was banished and American comics were not seen in Australia for thirty years (Coleman 1974, p. 108).

The feminist desire to censor popular culture is hardly a new story. From its inception, the Australian women's movement has been intimately involved in the history of censorship. The last two decades of the nineteenth century saw the emergence of a vigorous women's movement, the growth of the yellow press (the prototype of what we now call tabloid media) and the advent of obscenity acts in every state and colony.

So what can feminists today learn from the historical intersection of debates about women's rights, the supposedly corrupting influence of mass media and popular culture, aesthetic distinctions between literature, art and pornography and the ethics of sexuality? Quite a lot, as I hope to show in this chapter. There are some recurring patterns along with some important new wrinkles.

The history of censorship in Australia is an intriguing and complex story. People do not line up neatly in pro- and anti-censorship camps according to traditional political leanings or any other stable sign. Feminists themselves have been weaving back and forth across the censorship line for more than a century. But then, the feminist debate about censorship is interesting precisely *because* of its volatility—it's a magnifying glass positioned over a series of incendiary issues.

'Censorship and the mass media' is also a field which a broad group of disciplines and institutions want to stake a claim to. Lawyers, politicians, priests, philosophers, psychiatrists, art critics, media columnists—when it comes to hard-core pornography and low-brow television no-one wants to admit to reading or seeing it, but everyone's a critic.

Australia is a fortuitously contradictory place from which to view both feminism and censorship. The second country in the world to give women the right to vote in national elections, Australia was still banning us from pubs in the mid-1970s. And while Australians are notoriously sceptical of 'God-botherers' or 'wowsers' of any persuasion who might tell them how to run their lives, its citizens have in practice lived with one of the strictest censorship regimes in the Western world—a regime which is currently being reassembled after a brief lapse in the 1970s and early 1980s.

The Federal *Custom's Act* of 1901 was little used until 1929 when, according to Coleman, the federal government felt encouraged by a series of resolutions calling for censorship of immoral literature by 'church bodies, women's clubs, social groups, ex-servicemen's clubs and parents' organisations' (Coleman 1974, p. 13).

The banning of James Joyce's *Ulysses* in April of 1929 ushered in a censorship binge. By 1936, the list of prohibited publications comprised 5000 books and included Daniel Defoe's *Moll Flanders*, Aldous Huxley's *Brave New World*, George Orwell's *Down and Out in Paris and London*, Ernest Hemingway's *Farewell To Arms* and Radclyffe Hall's *The Well of Loneliness*. In 1930, the New South Wales Collector of Customs summarised the broad discretionary power of censorship given to customs officers when he told the *Sydney Morning Herald* that the department's test was 'whether the average householder would accept the book in question as reading matter for his family'. The use of the male pronoun leaves no doubt about who the law was meant to shelter most—women and children.

It wasn't until the late 1950s, that the Federal Customs Department signalled some relaxation of its strict censorship policies by announcing an intention to refer works of literature to a censorship board. In 1968, the Literature Censorship Board was replaced by a National Literature Board of Review, in the interests of bringing some uniformity to the decisions of the states. Then in 1969, Don Chipp became Minister for Customs in a federal Liberal government and ushered in a new unprecedentedly liberal period.

The federal government, however, was not the only enforcer of censorship, and it concerned itself largely with imported material. Locally produced books, magazines and newspapers were the province of state police departments—a state of affairs which has led to some predictably absurd seizures. In December 1930, for instance, the fine-arts magazine *Art in Australia* was seized after an enterprising bookseller advertised it as containing 'pictures for men only'. And in Adelaide, the publisher of 'Angry Penguins', Max Harris, had to defend the decency of a series of Ern Malley poems which were originally written as a hoax. The fact that the authors of the material, Harold Stewart and James McAuley, deliberately wrote the poems using arbitrary phrases and with an intentional disregard for any theme didn't stop the South Australian police and the magistrate in the case from uncovering salacious references in the work.

The Harris obscenity trial transcript brims with examples of the absurdities of allowing the police and the judicial system to act as de facto literary critics. In one famous exchange, prosecution witness Detective Vogelsang gave evidence that a poem entitled 'Night Piece' was obscene because it was set in a park at night. He said: 'I have found that people who go into parks at night go there for immoral purposes. My experience as a police officer might, under circumstances, tinge my appreciation of poetry' (Coleman 1974, p. 32).

FEMINISTS AND FREETHINKERS

A loose alliance of movements formed at the end of the nineteenth century, which included the movement for secular education; the republican movement; and the movement for birth control and the free discussion of sexual and moral questions. Their adherents were sometimes collectively known as freethinkers. From a feminist perspective, the movement is particularly interesting because some of its activists based their anti-censorship stance on the belief that equality for women was dependent on access to information about contraception and reproduction.

A book which figured prominently in censorship battles of the late nineteenth century was Charles Knowlton's *The Fruits of Philosophy*, which famous suffragette and population control advocate Annie Besant collaborated in publishing in the United Kingdom in 1877. The book included information about birth control, sexual pleasure and pregnancy and Australian booksellers were routinely fined for selling it. Like other books of this genre—Annie Besant's *The Law of Population* and George Drysdale's *Elements of Social Science* being two of the best known—*The Fruits of Philosophy* was often understood to be and sold as pornographic literature. In the sex-and-crime obsessed yellow press of the day it was common to find advertisements for bookshops specialising in pamphlets on contraception.

In a typical seizure incident in 1884, the police raided a Sydney bookshop and seized both Knowlton's and Drysdale's books. A senior police official who gave evidence against the bookseller described the books as 'the most obscene books to have come under his notice' and claimed they condemned chastity in women, advised girls to disregard virtue and eulogised prostitution (Coleman 1974, p. 51). A freethought conference which was in session at the time passed a resolution condemning the ongoing seizure of *The Fruits of Philosophy* and participants found support from the *Bulletin* which editorialised: 'There is no indecency in propounding in good faith a philosophy or social system which fails to penetrate the intellect of a Methodical Inspector of Police' (*Bulletin*, October 11, 1884).

The following year the police prosecuted Thomas Walker, a freethinker and advocate of population control who gave public lectures on contraception. Walker effectively fought the charge on the basis that he wasn't making any financial gain out of possessing 'obscene' diagrams. This legal victory paved the way for an important political victory for free-thinkers in 1888, when Judge Windeyer delivered a judgement vindicating birth control literature in *Ex parte Collins*. The case concerned a freethought advocate who was convicted of selling Besant's *The Law of Population*. In a landmark judgement, Windeyer rejected the classic Hicklin test of obscenity, according to which a book could be judged obscene if it was liable to corrupt the immature (that is, women and children) or the uneducated (the poor).

Windeyer's judgement had an immediate and broad impact on the availability of birth control literature. Indeed, there were few attempts to regulate this material again until the 1930s, when the broad distribution of leaflets advertising particular brands of contraceptives and abortion services caused a sufficient public outcry to result in a range of state laws banning such ads.

The real significance of Windeyer's judgement lies in the link he made between the basic human rights of women and their access to information about birth control. He wrote: 'What of the woman who is married to some unemployable drunk who treats her as a slave and who has already more children than she can feed or clothe? Why should she not use contraceptives?' (1888, 9 LR NSW 497).

In making this connection, Windeyer was taking a prominent stand in a contentious debate about the rights of women and the familial duties of men. As Australian feminist historian Marilyn Lake points out in her essay on the politics of masculinity in the 1890s, family desertion, domestic violence, unwanted pregnancy and male alcoholism were such serious social problems in the late nineteenth century they were considered a national crisis. Women's vulnerability to assault and poverty was exacerbated by the large size of the average family—eight children in 1870— and the limited economic independence of women. Lake comments:

Women's adult lives drained away in a series of pregnancies, miscarriages, births and periods of lactation. Earning an independent income in these circumstances was never easy . . . Increasing numbers of women found themselves juggling work and child care, in some cases because they left home and in others because their husbands abandoned them (Lake 1993, p. 9).

Early feminists had good cause to be concerned about the egregious effects male drinking and sexual promiscuity had on the lives of women. But their concerns were not solely rooted in the social and economic welfare of women—improving the moral health of the community was high on their list. Many feminists saw spiritual regeneration as the key to social reformation. The sanctity of maternity and the need to curb the natural brutality of the male sexual instinct were recurrent themes in feminist writings of the period. In 1894, the president of the Womanhood Suffrage League of New South Wales, Maybanke Wolstoneholme, wrote that prostitution, adultery, baby-farming, abortion, divorces and the harm done by romantic 'paper-covered serials' were 'undermining the sacredness and the beauty and the usefulness of the permanent marriage tie . . . made in the Heaven of man's higher nature, which all pure men and women desire to establish' (Sheridan 1993, p. 117). Even the campaign for female suffrage was sown on high moral ground. The Australian Woman's Christian Temperance Union, which led the suffrage cause in Australia, based its claim for women's right to vote on the argument that women's 'self-reliance' would result in 'a higher tone of social purity' (Evans 1977, p. 60).

In recent years, a number of feminist historians have tried to rescue the early feminists from an image of narrow-minded middle-class moralism. Lake, for instance, argues that the ideal of the independent, freewheeling bohemian immortalised in the *Bulletin* magazine of the 1890s, was premised on the social and economic subservience of women. 'The bohemians regarded their sexual attitudes as libertarian, but failed to notice that women's experience of the (male) "sex act" was often anything but pleasurable and frequently fraught with danger' (Lake 1993, p. 5). As a result, Lake claims, it's simplistic to dismiss feminist social purity campaigners as repressed moralists (or wowsers in Australian venacular). She writes:

> The material basis of women's receptivity to the feminist message was their role in reproduction; *their* workplace was the home . . . To depict women's concerns with temperance and social purity in terms of 'respectability' is to ignore the sexual politics; to describe the campaigners as Wowsers is to stigmatise them in the language of their masculinist enemies (Lake 1993, p. 11).

Lake is right to point out that the portrayal of late-nineteenth century feminists as uptight puritans assumes the universal availability of a libertarian lifestyle and ignores the rigidly gendered nature of social and economic life in the period. Nonetheless, the high moral rhetoric and the social purity agenda which dominated the early women's movement in Australia *is* relevant to an understanding of the historical relationship between feminism and censorship. Importantly, it points to the central role the liberal values of self-restraint and self-improvement played, and continue to play today, in the feminist debate about sexual ethics.

MENTAL RUBBISH FROM OVERSEAS

In 1957, a British magazine was successfully prosecuted in the Victorian courts for publishing two articles: 'I went to a "Sex Key" Orgy' and 'Unmarried Mother By Choice'. Condemning the second piece, one judge argued that it invested 'with an air of courageous and worthwhile social experiment a professedly deliberate flouting of the established moral and legal standards of the community . . .' (*Mackay v. Gordon & Gotch Ltd* 1959 ALR, 953).

The case illustrates an important distinction in the history of feminism and censorship—the difference between a paternalistic, liberal critique of censorship and what might be loosely termed a libertarian approach. From the freethought movement of the late nineteenth century to 1960s scholars who argued that *Portnoy's Complaint* had literary merit, liberals have been as quick as religious conservatives to draw the line at mass culture.

Windeyer's landmark judgement is, in fact, a perfect example of the paternalism embedded in the liberal pole. As Coleman writes of the judge: 'He saw moral criticism as valuable only so far as it increased the world's purity . . . It seems likely he would have regarded books advocating free love as obscene' (Coleman 1974, p. 57). This interpretation of the implicit limits to free speech on sexuality and reproduction is supported by a series of judgements in the 1950s, which refused to extend the Windeyer position to articles in the tabloid or popular press.

At the heart of the judicial opinions in these cases is the (still popular) view that it's one thing to disseminate educational information about sex and reproduction for high-minded social reasons, but it's quite another thing to publish it for entertainment. The same ideological split between high- and low-culture formats can be found in the argument that descriptions of sexual acts are OK if they occur in works of literature, but degrading if they crop up in porn magazines.

Campaigns to censor or ban mass cultural forms—from

the penny-dreadful romance and crime novels of the nineteenth century to the latest Sega video game—have been so
numerous in source, scope and object that it is impossible to
even sketch a history here. But it's important to note that
these campaigns do not readily divide along traditional political lines—liberals and conservatives frequently find
themselves in bed together. The 1930s Australian crusade
against American comics, is a good example of a campaign
which brought together commercial interests, nationalists,
local writers and artists' unions, racists, religious groups,
educators and liberals. The campaign had its origins in duties
imposed by Canadian and British customs on remaindered
American comics, which resulted in a flood of cheap comics
into Australia. The first to complain, not surprisingly, were
those directly economically affected—British comic book
publishers who traditionally sold only current issues to the
Australian market. But the economic rationale was quickly
overshadowed by the moral panic which ensued. A powerful
coalition of women's groups, church bodies and professional
organisations lobbied the minister for customs to variously
prohibit, tax or censor the magazines. To give some idea of
the wrath incurred by the Yankee scourge, the lobby included
the Australian Women's National League, the National Council of Women of Australia, the Housewives' Association of
New South Wales, the Women's Vigilant Society, the Woman's Christian Temperance Union, the New South Wales
Federation of Parents and Citizens, a number of state Coun-
cils of Churches, the Australian National Secretariat of
Catholic Action, the Parents' National Education Union, the
Australian Journalists' Association and the Children's Court

Magistrates' Association of Victoria (Coleman 1974, pp. 106–11).

The xenophobia and outright racism, which has historically shadowed concerns about cultural imperialism, is more than evident in a passage from a pamphlet, *Mental Rubbish from Overseas*, excerpted by Coleman. In reference to comic book stories, which, it claims, are influenced by African–American culture as well as the 'illiterate and superstitious peoples of Central and Southern Europe' who migrated to the United States, it states: 'The negro and his African jungle form no part of our national heritage and consciousness, and we will not have him here, neither in person nor by proxy through the permeation of his culture' (Coleman 1974, p. 109). The pamphlet was published by the Sydney Cultural Defence Committee, a left-wing organisation aligned with the Fellowship of Australian Writers.

The outcry finally resulted in federal customs regulations which gave the minister broad discretion to ban the comics. By September 1938, 73 had been prohibited and with the outbreak of World War II the entire trade was stopped. American comics only made their reappearance in Australia in 1960.

ANNUS MIRABILIS

Sexual intercourse began
In nineteen sixty-three
(Which was rather late for me)—
Between the end of the *Chatterley* ban
And the Beatles' first LP.

Philip Larkin, *Annus Mirabilis*

Larkin's stainlessly bleak ode to the sexual revolution is sometimes quoted in an effort to conjure the liberated spirit of the sixties. It's a use which entirely misses the poet's point. Larkin isn't hailing the sexual revolution as an authentic break with a dark and ignorant past. He's mocking the decade's self-congratulatory belief that it ushered in a new, more enlightened approach to sexuality. Larkin is hardly a fair-minded critic of liberal ideology. But his poem certainly fingers an important feature of the sixties censorship revolution—the smugness which attended the idea that society was emerging from a sexual dark ages into a bright health-giving light.

The sixties sexual revolution popularised a new truth about censorship: erotic literature wasn't sick or brutish, those who attempted to repress it were. And in prudish Australia, where even *Playboy* stayed banned until 1968, there was no shortage of ill-educated customs officials, wowserish priests and philistine politicians to mock.

A key plank of sixties liberal reform was the notion that censorship, as the *Sunday Mail* put it as early as 1934, was perpetuated by 'fussy old-womanish people who regard Australians as mental infants' (*Sunday Mail*, July 8, 1934). This image of censors as overprotective parents who refuse to cut the apron strings reached a crescendo by the late 1960s, when it became intertwined with the fear that Australia's censorship laws were promoting an image of the nation as culturally backward. This nexus is succinctly captured by Geoffrey Dutton and Max Harris in *Australia's Censorship Crisis*. They wrote of 'an urgent public feeling that censorship procedures and current actions in all the art forms do not accord with the "community standards" now held by the young and yet mature majority of Australians who are determined that this country shall enjoy the same cultural freedom in the same kind of way as other Western democracies . . .' (Dutton & Harris 1970, p. 6).

Dutton and Harris's argument highlights another important plank of the sixties liberal censorship reform agenda—it was based on the argument that the average contemporary person is 'mature' enough to handle erotic material and to decide what is fit for consumption and what is intellectually or morally worthless. Sixties liberals, in other words, simply wanted to transfer responsibility for deciding what was morally corrupting and what wasn't from police officers to individuals.

The sixties liberal argument, then, was most emphatically *not* an argument for doing away with the policing of the boundaries between acceptable erotica and harmful pornography. On the contrary, it's an argument that adults can be trusted to do the policing themselves. John Tasker illustrated this position admirably when he wrote in 1970: 'In civilised society, there is surely no reason for censorship. Pornography is boring to a well-adjusted adult . . .' (Tasker 1970, p. 49). This distinction between erotic literature and art (which portrays sex and sexuality in a healthy, balanced way) and pornography, (which reveals an unhealthily prurient, immature fascination with sex) recurs throughout the sixties debate.

(Liberals make unreliable defenders of free speech precisely because their defence is based on the ability of individuals to police their exposure to pornography. They often reverse their position later in life and argue things have gone 'too far' and people can no longer be trusted to keep themselves in check. In a 1973 preface to a book about censorship he originally wrote in 1961, for instance, Coleman questions the ongoing viability of his own liberalism and writes: 'What began as a movement for the spread of freedom, culture and knowledge has become a bandwagon for barbarians' (Coleman 1974, p. 1). Richard Neville, famous for his anti-censorship stands as an editor of *Oz* magazine, recently decried the potential harm caused to children by popular culture.)

The sixties liberal position did not gestate overnight. It had its roots in a libertarian ideology which was perhaps most infamously propounded by the Sydney University Professor of Philosophy, John Anderson. Anderson used the Freethought Society he helped found at Sydney University as a platform to oppose literary censorship in the 1930s and 1940s. He tied the banning of James Joyce's *Ulysses* to 'the central place of sexual repression in any repressive system, the way in which fear of sexuality carries over into fear of social disorder' (Coombs 1996, p. 9). Anderson was a mentor to a number of the founding members of the Sydney Push, a bohemian network of the 1950s and 1960s dominated by libertarians.

As Anne Coombs writes in *Sex and Anarchy: The Life and Death of the Sydney Push*, the men and women of the Push lived out the sexual revolution a good fifteen years before it hit the rest of society. Those associated with it tended to oppose the State, religion, censorship and monogamy. But their revolutionary activities were limited and, according to Coombs, they spent most of their time talking, drinking and gambling. The late Push, however, spawned a more activist breed of non-conformists, who included future feminists Liz Fell, Wendy Bacon and Germaine Greer (Coombs 1996).

By 1969, the centre of libertarian politics had moved to the University of NSW, where Wendy Bacon and a group of anarchist students were calling for the abolition of the Students Representative Council (SRC). Their opponents pointed out that the SRC provided necessary student services, including the publication of a weekly newspaper. Bacon and her colleagues responded by producing their own journal—*Thorout*. For Bacon, it was the beginning of a brief but notorious career in publishing. Her collaborators included Liz Fell, Frank Moorhouse, cartoonist Jenny Coopes and fellow editors Val Hodgson and Alan Rees. The magazines they worked on, variously titled *Tharunka*, *Thor* and *Thorunka*, were constantly under fire from the censor. Bacon says she and her fellow publishers, writers and artists set out to oppose the traditional liberal view that sexually explicit material was only acceptable if it had literary merit. Defending herself against a charge of selling obscene material in 1972, she argued that community standards were an illusion because what is obscene to one person can easily be a joke to another.

By the early seventies, however, the libertarian-anarchist ideology was being overtaken by other political forces. Germaine Greer's *The Female Eunuch*, Shulamith Firestone's *The Dialectic of Sex* and Julie Mitchell's *Women's Estate* became available in Australia in 1971. As Anne Coombs records, the women of the Push did not rush to join the burgeoning women's liberation movement—partly because they saw themselves as already liberated (Coombs 1996, p. 258). Wendy Bacon remembers the early seventies as a time when many women in her circle experienced a conflict between their libertarian instincts and the emergent feminist critique of pornography. She recalls being present in 1970 when a number of Women's Liberation Movement activists tore up copies of a *Tharunka* issue featuring a naked woman on its cover. Bacon remarks that many libertarian women viewed the radical arm of the emerging women's movement as 'part of the book-burning movement'. By the mid-seventies though, the vast majority of women associated with the Push were defining themselves as feminist rather than libertarian. Nonetheless, libertarianism left its fingerprints on an important strand of Sydney feminism and on the views and values of a number of significant Australian feminists. They include Germaine Greer, Liz Fell, Gillian Leahy, Eva Cox, Wendy Bacon, Anne Summers and Meaghan Morris. In an interview for this book Morris commented: 'Even for someone like me, who came into feminism from Marxist circles, libertarian culture was a pervasive horizon and a positive force . . . Nobody I knew in feminist circles wanted to go backwards. It was inconceivable that criticising the libertarians meant reinvoking censorship.'

By 1970, popular opinion on censorship had shifted sufficiently across the board to embolden Liberal Minister for Customs Don Chipp to condemn censorship with the fervour many of his counterparts had directed at sexually explicit material. Although he was eulogised at the time for going out on a limb—'a censor who dances to the music from "Hair", reads Dostoevsky, likes films and actually attends the Melbourne film festival' (Hall & Hall 1970, p. 27)—Chipp was in essence espousing a liberal position which had changed little since the nineteenth century. He might dip into D. H. Lawrence, but he was predictably appalled by the 'hard-core' pornography customs officials were obliged to sift through, such as the Swedish magazine he cited with 'page after page of close-up photographs of women holding their vaginas open with their fingers' (Hall & Hall 1970, p. 27).

A book which offers a glimpse at popular debate in this era is James and Sandra Hall's glossary of the censorship debate, *Australian Censorship: the XYZ of Love*. Poised on the cusp of two eras, this book came after the popularising of liberal anti-censorship campaigns but before feminist ideas gained currency in the mainstream. An extended passage on the legality of bare breasts in film includes the following: 'Though man-directed, the revolution in breast attitudes has been consistently supported by the younger woman. Her tenacity and daring has helped to convince the censors that breasts, black and white, are too beautiful to hide' (Hall & Hall 1970, p. 23). The largely unspoken assumption which animates the book is that sexual desire is largely male, hence a chapter heading 'G is for Girl, without whom there would be no censorship'.

As late as 1970, the Halls could write that advertising 'qualifies for inclusion in any discussion of censorship because in Australia it is rarely a victim of it' (Hall & Hall 1970, p. 8).

WOMEN AGAINST PORNOGRAPHY

In an ad for antidepressants from the early seventies a pretty woman in a gingham headscarf bites her nails and stares anxiously out from behind a phalanx of brooms and mops.

The copy reads: 'You can't set her free. But you can help her feel less anxious'. In 1972, one of Australia's largest advertising firms, George Patterson, released a report which summed up the female market this way:

> Above all, the average woman is a mother, and her whole life revolves around this basic role . . . As a good mother, she must also be a good wife and, basically, a good homemaker. Her home and family is the basis of her life; they are her domain. They are the justification of her existence . . . Her roles as mother and home-maker virtually define her very identity (*Patterson Report*, March 1972, p. ii).

You wouldn't know it from the analysis above, but second wave feminism had already caught fire across the Western world by the early seventies.

In Australia, its origins lay in two broad factions. One, a liberal, equity focused movement, had much in common with the United States National Organisation for Women, founded in 1966 by women who had served on President Kennedy's Commission on the Status of Women. This strand of feminism emerged in Australia under the auspices of the Women's Electoral Lobby (WEL). From the outset liberal or equity feminists were committed to working within existing legislative, governmental and judicial frameworks, as well as through the media, to improve social and economic conditions for women and fight discrimination.

The other loose coalition of interests emerged under the banner of the Women's Liberation Movement (WLM) in the late 1960s. While WLM intially attracted a diverse cross-section of women, including union activists and married women agitating to re-enter the workforce, its roots lay in the civil rights movement of the 1960s and the radical student left. Influenced by diverse strands of socialism and Marxism, WLM was self-consciously political in both theory and strategy from the outset and highly suspicious of the efficacy of 'working within the system'.

Beatrice Faust gives her version of the standoff between the two groups in her book *Backlash? Balderdash!*

The Revolutionaries, which include most Women's Liberationists, initially believed that women are pretty well entirely good and men are near enough to entirely bad and there can be no rapprochement between them. Women can only be liberated by overthrowing the oppressor—if they could only identify him or it. Finding that the revolution was nowhere in sight, some of them joined the establishment. In her Revolutionary days, Dr Anne Summers could not tolerate WEL meetings because WEL had a committee and it sometimes sat on the platform. Eventually, Dr Summers advised the Prime Minister (Faust 1994, p. 14).

Anne Summers also addresses the politics of this shift in the updated version of *Damned Whores and God's Police* (Summers 1994, pp. 505–29, see chapter eight).

From the outset, second wave feminists were overtly concerned about media representations of women. Debates about the significance of pornography and of sexist images in the media in general percolated through theoretical debates and activist strands in the Women's Liberation Movement. Rosemary Pringle recalls that 'the powder keg that pushed women to confront the issue of pornography' was the 1975 United States screening of the notorious film *Snuff* (Pringle 1981, p. 3). The film, which was billed as showing the actual rape, torture and murder of an actress, caused an outcry among feminists internationally and led to the formation in the United States of the influential Women Against Pornography group.

The reaction to *Snuff* illustrates the way the pornography debate was dominated from the outset by a tendency to imbue certain media images and texts with mythic, demonic qualities. The belief that *Snuff* shows a real woman being mutilated is still common today. Yet the film, now available on video in the United States, is actually a standard B-grade splatter movie, characterised by obviously amateur special effects. It's one thing to argue that videos which portray women being killed or maimed are evidence of misogyny, but it's quite another to claim that a widely distributed film shows the murder of an actual person. Ironically, the widespread campaign against *Snuff* has probably been responsible for a lot more anxiety and fear among women than the video itself, which is more likely to put the average contemporary viewer to sleep.

Some feminists involved in the antiporn agitations of the day were not unaware of the peculiarities of the time. Writing in 1981, Pringle remarked that 'almost in spite of ourselves we've been obsessed with porn, at least in Sydney recently. There have been radio programmes, meetings, a demonstration against the exhibition by Playboy at the Hogarth Gallery, and a viewing of porn organised by the Sydney Scarlet Woman collective at the Film-Makers Cinema . . .' (Pringle 1981, p. 3).

A 1980 article by Sue Wills and Joyce Stevens illustrates

a common critique at the time. In the course of the piece, the authors detail the horrors they encountered on a trip to Kings Cross to view porn 'in preparation for a recent Sydney Women's Liberation conference':

> The shorter movies make no pretence at having a story line—the prostitute, the dentist who fucks as he drills, the music teacher, the exotic cabaret—simply foils for non-stop fucking . . . What struck us most about the movies was their total unreality. The participants showed no flagging interest after hours of thrusting and probing, no failed erections, no premature ejaculations, no inhibitions, no bodies less than perfect, no bad breath . . . (Wills & Stevens 1980, pp. 3–4).

By the time the above piece was written, however, a schism was already developing between academic feminists whose ideas were being influenced by poststructuralist debates and public policy feminists who were keen to take an agenda based on values forged in the seventies into the public policy arena. I'll explore this crucial split more fully in chapter eight. For the moment, what I'd like to note is the more nuanced approach to sexual images in the media that begins to emerge in academic feminist writing at the time, as illustrated by an article penned only a year later by Elizabeth Grosz. In it she explored feminist ambivalence about the relationship between pornography and female sexuality, observing:

> Probably one of the most frequent comments in feminist discussions—at least the ones I've attended—is a confession on the part of a number of women that, despite the fact that they know pornography is 'ideologically

unsound', they still feel turned on or vaguely aroused by watching, reading or listening to pornographic materials (Grosz 1981, p. 16).

Grosz goes on to reject the argument that getting turned on by porn is simply a sign that women have internalised patriarchal ideology. Instead, she uses the porn debate as a jumping off point for exploring the feminist investment in high moral ground.

From its inception, the Women's Liberation Movement was a loose coalition of interest groups and, by the late seventies, it had radically fractured in both intellectual and activist terms. As a result, it's impossibly reductive to talk about a feminist 'position' on pornography or censorship emerging from this arena. But the fact that the debate about pornography and 'sexist' media imagery originated in radical, university-based elements of the Australian feminist movement *is* relevant to understanding its development and contemporary face.

In populist terms, the residue of the radical arm of the feminist movement has been more readily associated with a form of feminism which promotes the paradoxical claim that women are at once spiritually stronger and morally superior to men and, at the same time, destined to live as victims in the eternal shadow of patriarchy. In this framework, images which sexualise women are seen as the product of an intrinsically objectifying and violent male sexual drive which is foreign to the consensus-driven, loving and holistic sexual instincts of women.

The notion that pornography and sexist media images are a manifestation of male sexual aggression and violence towards women proved an emotionally powerful tool for channelling female rage and frustration about rape, sexual harassment and domestic violence. As public recognition of the extent of these practices grew, so too did the feeling of powerlessness and anger among those dealing with women who had been traumatised by these experiences. Andrea Dworkin, a United States feminist who has been influential in the antipornography movement internationally, sums up this deep sense of impotence:

It has plagued us to try to understand why the status of women does not change . . . Laws change but our status stays fixed . . . Rape, battery, prostitution, and incest stay the same in that they keep happening to us as part of what life is: even though we name the crimes against us as such and try to keep the victims from being destroyed by what we cannot stop from happening to them. And the silence stays in place too, however much we try to dislodge it with our truths. We say what has happened to us, but newspapers, governments, the culture that excludes us as fully human participants, wipe us out, wipe out our speech: by refusing to hear it. We are the tree falling in the desert. Should it matter: they are the desert (Dworkin 1993, p. 532).

By the 1980s, in Australia, the United Kingdom and the United States, movements variously known as 'Reclaim the Night' and 'Take Back the Night' were drawing thousands of women on marches to protest male violence, rape and, significantly, sexist media images and pornography. Male sexuality in all its manifestations became an emotive target of these gatherings. The slogan 'All men are rapists' is a popular summation of the view that even apparently consensual heterosexual intercourse constitutes sexual assault because of the unequal power of the partners. And while it's not a position that appealed to all feminists by any means, it's certainly a position that became identified with feminism in the popular imagination.

Ironically, this equation reflects an argument that has been used countless times to justify the oppression of women: that men are naturally sexually aggressive and violent and that, in order to afford women protection from male sexuality and aggression, their symptoms need to be policed, censored and punished. Women in this scenario are so powerless they are even unable to give consent to sex with a man.

The moral indignation which dominated this pole of the feminist debate was frequently attacked as such by liberal feminists—Beatrice Faust being one of the most prominent examples. In the early 1980s, however, an interesting hybrid began to emerge which gave rise to the current mainstream pro-censorship feminist position—liberal feminists (who'd been largely disinterested in pornography) effectively hitched up with radical feminists in efforts to ban and regulate pornography. The hitherto unlikely alliance was in no small part facilitated by the work of United States antiporn activists, Andrea Dworkin and Catharine MacKinnon.

In her recent book, *Defending Pornography*, feminist and president of the American Civil Liberties Union Nadine Strossen traces the history of the Dworkin–MacKinnon alliance and tracks the penetration of their ideology into the public sphere. A key turning point, Strossen argues, was the equation made by the pair and their supporters between sexual harassment and pornography. Sexual harassment, as

Strossen acknowledges, is an issue which has deservedly garnered serious attention over the past decade by politicians, policy makers, the judiciary and the media. Catharine MacKinnon's 1979 work, *Sexual Harassment of Working Women: a Case of Sex Discrimination*, is widely credited with pioneering the notion that sexual harassment is a form of gender-based employment discrimination—a view of the law which was recently imported into the Australian federal *Sex Discrimination Act*.

In recent years, however, MacKinnon has been successful in stretching this concept of discrimination to her chief concern, pornography. Strossen notes:

> . . . when employers, campus officials, judges, and other policy makers accept the argument that pornography, in turn, is sexual harassment—as distressingly many have done—then, in effect, they have accepted the claim that pornography is gender-based discrimination. This is a backdoor way into the procensorship feminist camp (1995, p. 121).

The impact of this connection between the equation of pornography with sexual harassment and the equation of sexual harassment with sex discrimination cannot be underestimated. In Australia, it is the key ideological link which paved the way for many politicians, bureaucrats and equity-focused feminists to join forces with the antiporn movement they had previously distanced themselves from.

As a result of this nexus, in the 1980s the pornography debate moved out of the radical arm of feminism and into the arena of public policy and law. Feminists in Australia, Canada and the United States formed interest groups and alliances with other antiporn factions focused on institutional means to ban pornography, ameliorate its supposed egregious social effects and compensate its 'victims'. In Australia, the culmination of these efforts came with the banning of X-rated videos in all Australian states.

Three: Mindless violence, loveless sex and family values

The random deaths of 35 people in Port Arthur in early 1996 at the hands of a methodical gunman stunned Australians and drew global concern. A week after the shootings, the *Sydney Morning Herald* juxtaposed two front-page headlines: 'Tasmania Buries Its First Dead' and 'MPs Consider Clampdown on Broadcast Laws'. The story which followed the latter quoted the Minister for Communications, Richard Alston, saying he was 'seriously' considering proposals to tighten control on violent television. The journalist who wrote the article Tony Wright, cited unnamed 'media reports' in support of his claim the gunman was 'obsessed by violent videos' (Wright 1996).

The idea that violent videos are responsible for violent and horrifically antisocial acts is seductive and extremely common. Limbering up for his 1996 bid for the White House, United States Republican Senator Bob Dole took a blowtorch to the belly of popular culture. The entertainment industry, Dole told a fundraising dinner, was now engaged in the 'mainstreaming of deviancy'. 'A line has been crossed', he said. 'Not just of taste, but of human dignity and decency.' It's a line which is crossed 'every time sexual violence is given a catchy tune', whenever Hollywood movies promote 'mindless violence and loveless sex' and when companies such as Time Warner release 'music extolling the pleasures of raping, torturing and mutilating women'. Dole then divided popular music and films into two groups—'friendly to families' and 'nightmares of depravity'.

The sincerity of Dole's attack can be measured by his inclusion of Republican supporter Arnold Schwarzenegger's high-tech shooting spree, *True Lies,* in his 'family-friendly' list. A seasoned politician, Dole knows a no-risk populist strategy when he sees one. Condemning gangsta rap (a code word for poor black males) couldn't have cost him a single vote among conservatives; supporting gun control (which might have a real impact on homicide statistics) certainly would have.

Dole, of course, is in good conservative company when it comes to assaults on the morality of popular culture. In 1994, Pope John Paul II attacked television as a major threat to family life, saying it glorified sex and violence and recklessly spread false values. Challenging parents to 'simply turn the set off', the Pope said television spread 'degrading values by broadcasting pornography and graphic depictions of brutal violence'. In Australia, religious conservatives such as the New South Wales state MLC the Reverend Fred Nile and federal Senator Brian Harradine have been at the forefront of campaigns against sex and violence in the mass media. What's disturbing, however, is the support the far right is now getting in its family values agenda from the centre and the left.

In 1992, Australian Prime Minister Paul Keating claimed Hollywood film violence was infiltrating society and causing 'terrible child murders'. Expressing concern for his own daughters, aged 13, 11 and 7, he said they were 'at the age where they are being subjected to very explicit violence' on television. One movie had 'quite upset' his youngest daughter and his older children were at an age where violent media was a 'bad influence' on them. Mr Keating's references to his family place his concerns about the media squarely within a traditional paternalistic framework. The media represents the corrupting and dangerous forces of the outside world from which the Prime Minister's children—and by extension, all Australians as people in his executive care—need to be protected (Lumby 1994b).

Former scourge of the establishment, *Oz* publisher Richard Neville, who was prosecuted for producing an obscene magazine in the 1970s, has also been touting some reactionary views about pop culture of late. Railing against Peter Greenaway's film *The Cook, the Thief, his Wife and her Lover*, Neville argued that audiences have become 'psychically numb'. To claims that he's become a spokesperson for conservative forces anxious to bring back censorship, Neville says he is merely promoting debate. 'I still believe freedom is paramount but I didn't fight a variety of court cases here and overseas just so a lot of millionaires could get richer by putting on the screen something which has nothing behind it except, one, to entertain, and two, to play on a very cheap and nasty appetite for violence'. Like so many other recent media 'critics', one of Neville's chief concerns is the dehumanising effects of media culture on children. But despite protestations he's not aligning himself with social conservatives, Neville's claim that contemporary popular culture panders to people's worst instincts and corrupts our youth is every bit as reactionary as the Pope's ostrich-like television-phobia. Neville pays no attention to differences in genre, tone, visual language or context in the media products he condemns. In the opening paragraph of his article 'Kill Culture' he conflates the film *Romper Stomper* (which shows the futility of the skinhead violence it portrays), an unspecified phenomenon called serial savagery (real life or representational—it's hard to say), Stephen King's novels (which partake in the longstanding tradition of gothic horror) and Rodney King's beating (Neville, 1993, p. 25). It's astounding that someone who once published one of the best-known Australian satirical magazines now exhibits such blindness to all but the most literal reading of media images, popular films and books.

Far more disturbing than Neville's liberal *volteface* is the 'family values'-based alliance between the left and the right which has been forged with the help of some prominent public policy feminists. Emblematic of this link is an Australian Senate committee set up in 1991 to report on the proliferation of phone sex services in Australia. Over the next five years, the committee sought and was granted numerous extensions to its life so it could inquire into sexually explicit and violent material in a range of media, including film, pay TV and the internet. The public face of the committee, which consistently condemned erotica and pornography, was dominated by a disturbing alliance between feminist Senator Margaret Reynolds and conservatives Independent Senator Brian Harradine (who opposes abortion) and Liberal Senator John Tierney (who wants R-rated videos banned from the home).

As *Independent Monthly* reporter John O'Neill pointed

out in a 1995 article on censorship, an examination of the debates and recommendations of the committee shows that, despite its claim to be representing community views, it consistently preferred anecdotal evidence to more comprehensive research which produced findings with which its key members did not agree. A 1994 press release, inviting submissions to an inquiry into R-rated material on pay television spent more than a page establishing the international support for Senator Reynolds' statement that there is great community concern about the relationship between the availability of such material and increasing levels of violence in society, 'in particular, sexual violence'. In spite of the senator's claim, national research conducted by the Australian Broadcasting Authority (ABA) into community attitudes to R-rated material on pay TV found an 82 per cent approval rating for making such programs available. But the committee didn't like the results. It subsequently took every step to sideline the ABA's research and to discredit the findings of a national inquiry into violence which argued that there is no link between media violence and aggressive behaviour. The federal government has decided to maintain a ban on R-rated material on pay TV. Summing up the results of the Reynolds–Harradine–Tierney alliance, O'Neill wrote:

> . . . the problem for the clear majority of Australians who the ABA study suggests want R-rated material on pay-TV (and however many people over 18 may want access to more explicit computer and video games) is that they do not send submissions to Senate Committee inquiries. The Presbyterian Women's Association of Australia, the Women's Action Alliance, the Catholic

Women's League Australia Inc. and the Forum for the Promotion of Human Dignity do. And the committee is choosing to interpret the views of such groups, rather than the views of Australians as indicated by much wider polling, as evidence of 'community concern' which it is legally bound to take into account during its deliberations (O'Neill 1995, p. 66)

The committee's composition bears out feminist writer Meaghan Morris's observation that a coalition is emerging in Australia 'between the extreme right-wing Christian forces and the very nice, middle-of-the-road, Labor-voting feminist forces' (Morris, 1995). As United States experience shows, one of the problems of this kind of alliance for women is that it offers the fundamentalist right a rhetorical smokescreen for their conservative views on women and families. Here's Senator Brian Harradine, for instance, objecting to non-violent erotica: '. . . much of the X-rated material treats women as sexual commodities to arouse the sexual desire of its targeted audience and reduces persons to objects or occasions of sexual pleasure' (Australian Senate 1995, p. 1219).

On the face of it, Harradine's objection to X-rated material is perfectly in line with popular feminist objections. But his views on abortion and a range of other feminist issues make it clear that the senator's objections to women being treated as 'sexual commodities' flow from a religious and deeply paternalistic view of the female role.

Another common nexus between conservative and feminist rhetoric is the claim that violent and sexually explicit media is damaging children and contributing to the breakdown of the family. Liberal Party senator Hedley Chapman summed up this 'family values' view when he praised a new classification bill for exhibiting 'a commitment by the government to ensuring that community standards and family values are not usurped by the ever increasing flood of pornography and unacceptable material which seems to be creeping into every facet of life in Australia' (Australian Senate 1995 p. 1213).

This 'family values' rhetoric fits well with a moralistic and reactionary strain of maternalism which lies at the heart of pro-censorship feminism, and which endorses a vision of society in which right-minded feminists will act as de facto spiritual parents to the rest of us (with the aid of state power). The aim is to institutionalise the ethical values of a particular section of the feminist movement, using a combination of surveillance and discipline.

Because they often see themselves as social radicals, pro-censorship feminists usually protest when they're described as moralistic or authoritarian. Senator Margaret Reynolds, for instance, told an interviewer that she has 'absolutely no concern about erotica, and particularly erotica that is women's erotica and is from a woman's perspective . . . where erotica is about two people in mutual love-making'. She is only opposed to sexually explicit material which is 'all about some sort of mechanical act that is supposed to be sexual but you really wonder whether it isn't really some sort of gymnastics' (Huntley 1995).

The idea here seems to be that we'll be allowed to have access to sexually explicit material again when we've all been properly schooled in the higher feminist ethical understanding of human sexuality. When we've learnt to want erotica, not pornography. The problem is that notions of 'real' sexuality, like 'real' women or 'real' life, are inevitably grounded in coercive notions of what it means to be normal. And that's precisely the point at which pro-censorship feminism links back up with a religious, fundamentalist family values agenda.

PLAYING IN THE INFORMATION TRAFFIC

When radio news reported that a gang of teenagers had beaten a six-year-old boy (John Ashfield) into a coma, talkback lines caught fire. Talkback hosts and their callers demanded an end to the violent videos, films and television programs they had no doubt were responsible. It wasn't until the next day, after John died, that a different story came out. John's death was the result of a classic act of domestic violence which certainly predates the television era.

Three months later, in November of 1993, a United Kingdom trial judge passed sentence on two eleven-year-old boys found guilty of murdering toddler James Bulger. 'I suspect that exposure to violent video films may, in part, be an explanation', he said. Despite the absence of any police evidence to support his opinion, within hours the British Home Secretary was under intense pressure from fellow MPs and voters to ban video 'nasties'. British MP David Alton summed up popular sentiment when he tabled a motion calling for more control over the violent material which 'all too often saturates people's homes'. 'It is crucial', he said, 'that the nation searches its soul and asks how this kind of crime can happen and what are the causes of this unspeakable violence in our society'.

It's common wisdom that society is becoming more

violent and that there's a causal link between media depictions of violence and violence in the home and on the
streets. But according to the most comprehensive recent
report on violence and its causes in Australian society,
Australia's rate of homicide is relatively low by international
standards and hasn't changed significantly over the past
twenty years. The report also found that, despite popular
perception, violent offending by juveniles is uncommon,
gang violence is not a major problem and most homicides
and assaults are committed by someone known to the victim.
In fact, the age group most at risk of being murdered are
children under the age of 12 months (Australian Institute
of Criminology 1990). Statistics from the NSW Bureau of
Crime Statistics and Research released in 1996 suggest that
little has changed since the 1990 report. They show that the
annual homicide rate in Australia's most populous state has
been stable for the past 25 years and that there's been no
rise in the number of multiple murders.

When it comes to the causes of violence Professor
Duncan Chappell, who chaired the National Committee on
Violence, argues that media influences should go at the
bottom of a long list headed by family influence and economic inequality. 'The causes of violence are extremely
complex', he says, 'and we're not going to find any simple
answers even though many people would wish to'. According
to Chappell, the widespread concern about violent films,
videos and games is a result of people 'desperately searching
around for something to pin the blame on' (Lumby 1994c).
Chief censor with the Australian Office of Film and Literature Classification, John Dickie, agrees. 'There is a general
concern about violence all round', he says. 'And I think

because the media is there and often portrays violence people say "Ah yes, it's because of the media". Yet every report I've seen puts media influences at the bottom of the list of causes of violence. But the media is out there, it's available and it's easy to point the finger at.' (Lumby 1994d).

If research into the effects of violence in the media is evidence of anything, it's proof that the relationship between a given medium, its content and its viewers is unpredictable and complex. Police routinely announce that they've found violent or sexually explicit videos and books in the houses of serial murders or rapists—but then they could find similar material in the houses of many perfectly peaceful Australians. Images of violence circulate throughout popular culture, from morning cartoons, to the news, to action movies—yet research into violence shows no evidence that we're becoming a more violent society or that popular culture is prompting people to commit violent acts. What's more, an overview of international homicide statistics suggests that access to violent videos is not a deciding factor in levels of violent crime. Australia and Britain are both countries with substantially lower homicide rates than the United States and yet both countries are high consumers of US popular culture. The real variables are access to guns, the prevalence of an illegal drug trade and the levels and demographic concentration of poverty.

And even if there are a small handful of unstable people with violent tendencies who feel reinforced by watching *Rambo* films, it's unclear how tightening censorship laws will prevent them from finding other sources of vindication. What about terrorists who feel authorised to shed blood in the name of the Bible or the Koran? Or Croatians enraged by news footage from the Bosnian conflict? Banning images of violence from popular culture is an impossible task since violence pervades a wide range of genres and formats—many of them respected 'high culture' works in the literary and filmic canons. What's more, the relationship between representations of violence and real-life events is relentlessly circular. The Port Arthur massacre had no sooner occurred than it became part of a vast repertoire of stories about violence, dating back to cave paintings, Ancient Greek friezes and epic poetry. To blame actual violence on representational violence is bizarrely animistic. As McKenzie Wark writes in his essay 'Child's Play': 'The media show images of evil and violence in the world. Therefore the media must be the *cause* of the evil and violence in the world that the media then picture in still more images.' (Wark 1994, p. 88).

Rather than futilely wishing popular culture would disappear, those who are concerned that it will harm children would be much better off taking media and cultural studies seriously and promoting their inclusion in primary, secondary and tertiary curricula. Too often though, the very people who attribute the most powerful influence to popular culture are the least willing to see it taken seriously by educators and students. Recent Australian research into children and television violence, for instance, points to the important role parents play in teaching children to negotiate the meaning of television programs. Commenting on recent calls to ban violence from prime-time television, media scholar Lee Burton writes that:

Parents or older children can moderate the content of shows by reassuring children that 'it's only a story—it doesn't happen that way in our family' . . . It is the children with their own television sets or whose parents don't care what they watch that we should be concerned about. Putting violent shows on later would not change their situation. (Burton 1992, p. 20)

One of Burton's key insight here is the way diverse television viewing helps children learn how to negotiate media texts—an important skill in contemporary life. Eliminating violence from any show children are likely to watch (including, presumably, the news), in other words, makes as much sense as eliminating traffic from children's daily lives. Children need to learn to interact with the media—to distinguish the kinds of violence in drama, cartoons, comedy and on the news—in the same way they learn to cross the road. The fact that some children are neglected—effectively allowed to play in the information traffic—is not an argument for turning television over to endless *Andy Pandy* re-runs, but it may be a good argument for including popular culture in the school curriculum.

Another common idea, which is often coupled with the argument that violent images are making people more violent, is the idea that the mass media images are becoming increasingly violent. That even if *we're* good, our *popular culture* is bad—and unworthy of the quietly dignified moral majority who are drowning under the tidal wave of trash unleashed on them by corrupt Hollywood executives and media magnates.

Writing in *New York* magazine, Michael Hirschorn formulated a simple but effective response to the tidal wave theory—make a list of what's actually selling at the box office and on the box. The squeaky clean results Hirschorn wound up with, which included *Casper*, *Pocahontas* and *The Bridges of Madison County*, led him to pose a more salient question—is popular culture too wholesome? (Hirschorn 1995).

In 1993, commercial television networks across Australia moved to self-regulate their program content with a code of practice. Under the code, viewing is divided into four classifications corresponding to time zones: G, PG, M and MA. The type and levels of violence in a program determines which zone it can be shown in. For example, the code states that depictions of threatening language, weapons and special effects can be shown in a G zone (3.30 pm to 7.30 pm on weekdays) only if they are not 'likely to cause alarm or distress to children'. 'Sustained, relished or excessively detailed acts of violence' are banned from all time zones. Popular perceptions to the contrary, the code is right in line with a move towards a more vigilant approach to the censorship of violence generally and with an expanded role and budget for the Australian Office of Film and Literature Classification.

BEYOND THE STANDARD COMMUNITY

We have a [Film Review] Board that is highly unrepresentative. If you look at the occupations of the 10 people involved . . . they include journalists, film critics, teachers, lecturers in media studies, public servants, school counsellors and a fitter . . . I am sure these people are very learned in these matters relating to film but the question is: do they really reflect community standards? (Australian Senate 1995, p. 1211).

When politicians, such as John Tierney who is quoted above, advocate censorship they often claim they're not actually speaking for themselves, they're *responding* to an overwhelming community concern. The idea that censorship represents a line in the sand—a marker of community standards—is a classic liberal notion, based on the belief that democracy means achieving consensus from conflicting community interests. But feminists, social conservatives and lots of people in between have since adopted it as a justification for their own agendas.

Community standards *sound* solid and commonsensical enough—but as their defenders often discover, they can prove pretty elusive in practice. The history of censorship and pay TV in Australia illustrates this. Despite the 1994 Australian Broadcasting Authority survey that found that 82 per cent of people believed adults should have the right to watch R-rated material on pay TV, the federal government chose to listen to the contrary opinion of an eight-member Senate Select Committee on Community Standards instead. Why? According to the senate committee, the adults surveyed didn't really understand what R-rated material was, even though they were shown the Office of Film and Literature's guidelines which described the R rating in detail (O'Neill 1995, p. 64). The Senate Community Standards Committee effectively argued that the average member of the community lacks sufficient expertise to make a judgement about what they should be allowed to see on pay TV. It acted as if community standards are something governments and expert bodies ought to set.

Yet, some of the same committee members have attacked opponents of censorship for being too 'expert' and therefore out of touch with 'ordinary' people. In a 1995 interview Senator Margaret Reynolds contrasted the kind of 'intellectual, reasonable' people with whom she could debate Pasolini with people from 'the real world of suffering of women' (Huntley 1995). Reynolds clearly intended her remark as an anti-elitist gesture—a recognition that she is a member of privileged class. In fact, she's buying into a very hierarchical notion of culture.

The idea that academics who live in leafy middle-class suburbs are somehow outside reality because of their specialist knowledge misses the complexity of the way we all consume contemporary culture. Academics might be sipping Chardonnay and debating *Salo* one minute, but it's fairly likely they'll be watching Seinfeld, listening to rap music or settling back with a beer in front of the footy the next. Popular culture, including Pasolini films, Jane Austen novels and dance music, is diverse and contradictory—and so are the ways we interact with it.

Being media-literate isn't a matter of bringing 'superior' academic knowledge to bear on a television program or a video game (and thereby ensuring you won't be unduly influenced or affected by it). Media literacy demands involvement—it requires an intuitive understanding of the way different media texts interact. From television news and the newspaper op-ed page to billboard ads and music videos, the media is part of the language of everyday life—and like any language, there's a big difference between understanding it and actually *speaking* it.

More to the point, academics aren't the only people with opinions about the media. From workmates recounting a sitcom joke, to radio talkback callers frying a politician, friends arguing about the merits of Nicole Kidman's performance in *To Die For*, strangers at a barbecue discussing the O.J. Simpson trial or a fervent Labor supporter hurling a shoe at John Howard's grinning face on 'Lateline'—most people are quick to voice their views and discuss points of discomfort and identification with popular culture. This interaction is an important part of contemporary culture. The media might supply us with ideas about the world we live in, but it's also constantly soliciting our opinions and desires to ensure its survival. And in this sense we're all media producers. The notion of community standards is grounded in a set of assumptions which are out of touch with this dynamic aspect of contemporary culture. It assumes there's a coherent community to appeal to, which exists in isolation from the media and shares the same values and beliefs. And it denies the way many of us have learnt to juggle multiple identities.

Speaking at a public seminar on the banning of a queer film, *In A Glass Cage*, Meaghan Morris argued that it's time to move beyond the idea of community consensus to a system which acknowledges that 'films can be watched in many different ways by many groups of people'. Instead of focusing on censorship, distributors and producers should focus on giving people enough information so they can make a meaningful choice about whether they want to see the film or not. Giving power back to the consumers in this way, Morris argues, is part of 'negotiating livable rules of conduct between diverse communities that have to live together and yet have completely incompatible values or expectations about social life and conduct'. From a feminist point of view, adopting this stance means relinquishing a bid to *control* representations of women in favour of a strategy which ensures diversity in media product and information.

INVESTING IMAGES WITH MAGICAL POWER

In 1993, New South Wales Magistrate Pat O'Shane delivered a speech from the bench about violence and women in a male-dominated society. The catalyst was her decision to use her discretionary powers to record no conviction against five young women charged with malicious damage to a billboard. They defaced it because they believed the image promoted violence against women. How, Ms O'Shane asked, can property rights be compared to the right of women to live without fear of violence and sexual abuse? While she found the women were in breach of the law, Ms O'Shane effectively branded the advertisers the real criminals.

The strength of her feelings on the matter were obvious in an interview following the decision. She found it, she said, 'very, very difficult' to see the ad as doing anything other than inciting violence against women. She added: 'I would have some serious misgivings about any person who seriously argued that it could not be seen in that light, or should not be seen in that light. Women constitute 51 per cent of the population and I don't know any women in my areas of contact—and they're fairly broad-ranging—who accept that kind of advertising.'

The image in question—a Berlei lingerie ad—is based on a traditional magic trick in which a magician places a woman in a box and 'saws' the box in half. The main complaint about the ad is that it invites sexual violence against women because it shows a smiling, attractive woman being hacked in two and even suggests women enjoy this kind of torture by captioning the image, 'You'll always feel good in Berlei'.

A cursory inspection of the image suggests that this is a rather narrow reading of the ad. The cartoonishly wide, white, serrated perforation which suggests a sawing action, runs vertically through the entire poster, not merely through the woman. The image, in other words, plays its own visual 'trick' on the magician's trick—it is his magic act, not just the woman's body which has been 'cut' in two. Rather than showing a woman being sawn in two by a man, the ad actually shows a hokey magical scenario which has been reversed—turned against the magician. And, far from looking 'passive' as a number of complainants suggested, the woman in the picture is propped casually on one elbow, facing the camera and smiling knowingly—the implication is that *she*'s the one in charge of the trick.

My point here is not that the feminists who spray-painted the billboard read the image 'wrongly', but that the Berlei magic trick ad contains a cautionary tale for anyone who wants to impute magical powers of persuasion to ads. Contemporary advertisers tend to give consumers more credit than that. Aware they're dealing with an image-literate public, advertisers increasingly trade in images which acknowledge their status as images. The vertical 'tear' in the Berlei image calls attention to its status as a billboard ad—it looks like someone tore the whole poster in half—in the same way that using a woman as a magician's assistant in a cheesy magic trick acknowledges and satirises the traditional role of women as passive assistants and 'victims' of magicians.

Pat O'Shane's contention that she'd have 'serious misgivings' about anyone who disagreed with her reading of the ad is an attempt to replace one supposedly dominant cultural viewpoint (the patriarchal one) with another feminist reading. But what room does this strategy leave for recognising a shift in the dominant point of view? Isn't the feminist campaign against 'sexist' ads, in a sense, dependent on finding evidence of this dominant point of view everywhere? What would feminist politics look like if feminists unhitched themselves from the need to constantly *oppose* patriarchy and began to define their needs and desires outside these reactive terms?

In 1995 Calvin Klein was forced to curtail an ad campaign shot by photographer Steven Meisel on the grounds that it was 'kiddie porn'. The ads, shot in a deliberately amateurish style, were all set in a cheesily furnished suburban rumpus room—a setting which the ad critic of the US trade publication *Adweek* described as a 1970s retro look designed to 'recreate the back pages' of adult magazines of the era.

The teenage models in the ads lounge about wearing variously blank, sulky and enigmatic expressions and little more than underwear and the odd denim vest. Summing up the concern stirred up by the ads, one critic said the ads showed 'young people as whimsical sexual marionettes in the hands of adults'. Calvin Klein responded to his critics with a full-page statement in the *New York Times* which read in part: 'The message of the CK Calvin Klein Jeans current advertising campaign is that young people today, the most media savvy generation yet, have a real strength of character and independence . . . We are also conveying the idea that glamour is an inner quality that can be found in regular people in the most ordinary setting . . .'

Opposition to the Calvin Klein ads brought together a wide variety of groups, including child welfare authorities, feminists, leaders of the Catholic League and members of the highly conservative American Family Association. What's unclear is who, exactly, they were looking to protect—a question which prompts another: who are the ads meant to appeal to? And why have they drawn such demographically broad attention?

The age group portrayed in the commercials—boys and girls in their mid-teens—are, as Calvin Klein points out, media savvy and (at the time of writing) in the grip of a mid-seventies revival, a style which makes fashion sense out of the amateur-hour aesthetic of the CK campaign. In relation to this group of consumers, critics seem concerned the campaign is exposing them to overtly sexualised images of themselves or to intimations of an inappropriately adult sexuality.

There's a simple response to the claim that the ad will corrupt young adolescents and encourage them to flaunt their sexual power: teenagers *are* sexual beings. Across the Western world boys and girls are reaching puberty earlier than ever before (often before they reach their teens) and they are having sex younger. In North America, more than half of all teenage girls between the ages of 15 and 19 have had sex—double the rate in 1970. And five times as many 15 year olds are now sexually active (Pipher 1996, p. 207). If popular debate about teenage sexuality is any indication, it's not something many adults or parents are comfortable with. But it's not showing any signs of going away as a result. Rather than seeking to ban images which depict teenagers as sexually precocious, concerned adults might accomplish more by supporting the availability of quality sex education, contraceptives and personal counselling for high school kids. The latter would arguably do more to help teenagers deal with sexual approaches from adults than trying to bury all representations of the issue.

But if kids aren't the problem what about adults? What are we to make of the suggestion that these teenage models are being seduced by someone older—isn't this a legitimation of the sexual abuse of children by paedophiles? Given the strength of feeling in the community on this subject, it's a question which deserves a careful response (and one I consider in greater detail in chapter seven).

Perhaps the best way to address this question initially is to pose a series of other questions. What kind of fears or other uncomfortable emotions is the Calvin Klein ad campaign provoking in adults who don't engage in sex with children or teenagers? Is it common for such adults to sexualise teenagers? Are all sexual experiences between sexually mature teenagers and adults damaging? And, if they are, what's an appropriate response to this kind of desire? Will banning all images which conjure this aspect of human sexuality defuse it? And if one of the key concerns on the part of critics of the Calvin Klein campaign is that teenagers are naive and powerless in the face of adult sexuality, then isn't it better to encourage discussion of these issues than suppress them?

These aren't easy questions to answer, nor are they particularly easy to pose. But they do need to be considered if the debate about images of teenage sexuality is going to move beyond the simple victim scenario in which teenagers are constructed as the innocent and asexual potential victims of monstrous paedophiles.

On a less contentious note, another dimension of the CK campaign's appeal was its popularity with the thirty-something market. This campaign arguably had a very particular impact on this demographic group, since it was marketing their early adolescence back to them. The years immediately following puberty probably aren't many people's idea of a fun or glamorous time—what the Calvin Klein campaign did was to effectively repackage the awkward, nerdy, artlessness of mid-seventies adolescence and *make* a virtue of it. It elevated the seventies—and the matching-denimed teenagers we catch glimpses of in home movies—to a style.

My wider point here is that even a single advertisement speaks in many voices simultaneously and invokes a range of diverse desires (and fears) across the social spectrum. And, in this sense, a simple ad campaign is a microcosm of broader media culture—it is a fractured and contradictory text.

But even feminists who maintain popular culture remains absolutely dominated by a patriarchal point of view may be prepared to consider this: if feminism continues to build its popular politics *on* a simple opposition to a supposedly dominant patriarchal point of view, it's in great danger of simply reinforcing that point of view. As even an average advertising agency will tell you, negative advertising is *at best* defensive—it puts you on the map in relation to another product—at worst, it amounts to free advertising for the other camp.

Four: Consuming artifice

> The last guy I was with covered his naked penis with his hands and whined, 'Stop touching it' . . . We unanimously diagnosed this bizarre condition as postmodern performance anxiety . . . (*Future Sex*, 1994).

Spartan diets and stringent exercise regimes. Stomach-firming routines and buns-of-steel workouts. Fashion spreads and low-fat cooking tips. Guides to finding true love. Articles about pleasing your partner in bed, guilt-free masturbation and better parenting. Ads for dieting aids and plastic surgery. When it comes to narcissism, neurosis and sheer self-surveillance, *Cosmopolitan* and *Cleo* have got nothing on *Men's Health* magazine. A leading magazine in the burgeoning United States men's 'fitness' magazine market which is now available in Australia, *Men's Health* sells its readers a monthly hit list of male flaws and failings along with a punishing regime for addressing them. The standards are exacting—even sexual pleasure has got to be worked at. A 1995 article, for instance, reminds over-25 readers that now 'your early 20s are over, and those marathon lovemaking sessions are gone . . . it's easy to start wondering if the party's over libido-wise'. The solution? A rigorous and complex exercise regime aimed at 'getting fit for fooling around' and 'training your love muscles'. And, in case readers are thinking of slacking off after they've dominated in the sack, this guide to better sexual performance is buried between articles describing subsistence level diets, gruelling exercise regimes and penetrating personality primers.

The 1995 annual sex issue of *Details*, a contemporary US men's magazine distributed in Australia and aimed at the twenties and thirties inner-city male market, also makes a little bit of erotic pleasure sound like an awful lot of hard work. Good sex, according to an article on tantric sex, requires 'devotion, commitment and sacrifice', not to mention a couple of thousand bucks for an expensive course in how to do it. In the *Details* 'sexual IQ test', sexual competency emerges as a daunting array of knowledge about sexual terms, practices and devices. The lead article, a survey of 'the new landscape of sex and desire', warns that 'these days, no matter how you play, you pay'. And a forum on contemporary males poses a series of angst-ridden questions about the nature 'of that strange beast masculinity'.

Rival men's magazine *Esquire* posed the question: 'Do women actually love us or simply *tolerate* us?'. The discouraging response, diplomatically summed up by Nancy Friday, who chaired a five-woman inquiry into the issue was: 'I would hate to think that the anger in that room represents women at large'.

Anxiety about masculinity is rising off contemporary magazines aimed at a young male market like steam off a locker-room floor. From endless articles devoted to disciplining and beautifying the male body to (sometimes hostile) articles examining the meaning of feminism in contemporary society, the overriding message is that masculinity has entered an age of profound uncertainty. It's a far cry from the urbane, paternalistic world of *Playboy* circa 1960, in which the major questions troubling men were 'the correct storage and serving of liquor in the urban apartment' and how to get hold of an unexpurgated copy of *Lady Chatterley's Lover*.

Perhaps the single most striking change in contemporary men's magazines is the overt eroticising of the male body. While magazines such as *Esquire*, *Details* and *Arena* regularly profile attractive female celebrities, the great majority of naked bodies featured in editorial and advertising are male. And, in magazines like *Men's Health* and *Men's Fitness*, women have all but disappeared. From ads for cologne and mineral water, to the photo spreads accompanying feature articles, the focus is resolutely on the male form.

In Australia, one of the first images to sexualise the male body was an ad for Sheridan sheets, showing a muscled and tanned male torso swaddled in a set of suggestively rumpled sheets. In the same era, Bruce Weber's ads for Calvin Klein, featuring pretty, well-built adolescent boys, also caused debate. Today, toned and tanned nude male bodies are mandatory props in ads for a wide range of male products. The June 1995 edition of *Gentleman's Quarterly*, for instance, contained fourteen separate ads featuring naked men.

To understand all these rippled, oiled-up bodies as purely homoerotic is to misrecognise the kind of desire which flows between the media and its audience. Magazines, whether they are pitched at a nominally hetero or homosexual market, are all courting our desire to consume. Which prompts the question: consume what? The obvious answer is products. The things advertisers and merchants want us to buy: cars, cosmetics, condoms and cigarettes.

But contemporary consumers are hungrier than that. We're not satisfied with mere goods and services. We want everything associated with products too—or to put it another way, we'll turn almost anything or anyone into a product. Elle Macpherson, rugby league, the Nike logo, old Coca Cola bottles, the black and gold packaging which says Chanel No. 5, blond hair, Jane Austen, the internet. We don't just buy stuff—we buy the idea of stuff. We consume images.

And images are what the media is made of. When we flip through a magazine, the ads and the articles tend to merge. It's not so much a particular brand of computer or jeans which attracts us, it's the context. To appeal to late capitalist consumers, products literally need to develop a life of their own—a *style*. American model Cindy Crawford recently referred to this phenomenon as 'synergy'. Launching herself as the mascot for an upmarket brand of British luggage, Crawford told journalists that she'd agreed to take the job because the company was in synch with her image, and the image of the other goods she promotes.

Crawford is right about synergy. It's pretty difficult to say where Cindy the person stops and a leather suitcase begins. In between are a host of other products which include Cindy the Supermodel, Cindy the Girl Who Broke Richard Gere's Heart, Cindy the Girl Next Door and Cindy the *Playboy* Model. Images set up a chain reaction and it becomes hard to separate them from the product or thing they represent.

When we read magazines we consume images—which is different from buying magazines and the products in them. The new sexualising of the male body is more than the extension and refinement of an existing market for cosmetic goods or sports shoes—it's part of the growing order of commodification, which includes all of us. Rather than simply acting as lures for commodities—images have become desirable in themselves. Or, as I will argue in this chapter, our desires—and our very sense of self—are increasingly modelled on the logic of images.

CONSUMING OUR SELVES

It's a Marxist-feminist credo that social and economic conditions have forced women to turn themselves into objects of vision for men. Men look at women, the argument goes, and women learn to see themselves through the eyes of men. This process determines more than relations between men and women—it determines the way women relate to themselves. Women experience themselves as images designed to please an all-powerful male audience. They act out this image, even though it's in conflict with their 'real' selves.

The notion that representations or appearances are, at best, pale reflections of a reality located elsewhere and, at worst, deceptive and corrupting is persistent and ancient in the Western philosophical tradition, beginning with Plato's hostility to representational arts, like painting. Judeo-Christian theology is punctuated with warnings about the misleading power of images, from Moses' injunction against the Golden Calf, to Saint Augustine's condemnation of the ocular desire which diverts our minds from spiritual contemplation, to the iconoclasm of the Protestant Reformation.

Our image-saturated culture has inherited all the anxieties of a philosophical tradition that distrusts the very nature of the image. Our culture of images, in fact, calls into question the very concept of a 'real' self. It's not just women who are placed on display—all of us are watching ourselves from a distance, uncertain of where the representation stops and the self begins. No-one is exempt from the vast pop-culture image machine. Designer dykes, macho faggots, white-trash intellectuals, new-age suburbanites, yuppie bikers, young fogies, celebrity academics—the labels are as diverse as the products they are designed to promote. All of us have learnt to consume our selves.

SHOW US YOUR BUNS

I grew up in a hayseed town of five hundred people . . . I'm definitely a COSMO girl. Let me give you two examples:

1. I drive a rugged four-wheel drive pickup truck and a lipstick red Miata, because a COSMO girl knows you have to have the right tools for work *and* pleasure.
2. When I bring a new boyfriend to my little home-town, I'm always asked the same question: 'When are you kids getting married?' I just smile confidently and say, 'I'm not sure, I haven't asked him yet.'

(Australian *Cosmopolitan* August, 1995)

If contemporary young men's magazines fairly bristle with

sexual and emotional anxiety, advising men to 'lose that gut', cultivate 'abs of stone', and brush up on their cunnilingus ('Don't treat her vagina like an ice-cream cone' and 'Don't hum', according to *Gentleman's Quarterly*), their female counterparts vibrate with a different kind of tension. They trade in *attitude*.

Take *Cleo* magazine. Compare it, in fact, to *Men's Health*. Both magazines feature articles on romantic relationships, but *Cleo* takes a more sexually explicit approach—recent issues have featured graphic articles on anal sex, fellatio and masturbation. And while *Men's Health*, like most young men's magazines, is falling over itself to explain female desires to its readers, *Cleo* flaunts an openly cynical attitude to the opposite sex. An article entitled 'Why men cheat (apart from being dick-driven, that is!)' is a case in point.

Typical of this provocative tone is another article in a 1994 issue of *Cleo* on gunslinging female movie stars. After describing scenes in which scores of top female stars shoot and kill men, the article ends on the following note:

> To see America's favourite mousy TV good-guy rave like Charlie Manson and then receive a gut full of lead from Sciorra—to see Alan Alda get screwed, once and for all [a reference to the film *Whispers In The Dark*]—is one of recent moviegoings giddiest highs. How many loitering male dickheads in Hollywood deserve to be handled in just such a manner? Anyone's wish list would surely be as long as Geena Davis's legs. What are you women waiting for? (Atkinson 1994).

Substitute the word female for male in the above quote and it becomes unprintable in the mainstream media.

But it's not just *Cleo* magazine which uses the politics of resentment to boost readers' egos and sales. *Cosmopolitan* magazine, a common target of middle-class feminist derision for its supposedly conservative advice on handling heterosexual relationships, had this to say in a 1995 issue to women caught having affairs:

> . . . all of us are taught to be deeply sympathetic to men's vulnerabilities, particularly their sexual vulnerabilities; we are predisposed to accepting men's rage and men's punishment *at the mere suspicion of a woman's infidelity* . . . My advice is to *run* from anyone who says, in effect, 'You've been very bad, and now you must knock yourself out to return to goodness again' (Heyn 1995, p. 155).

Perhaps the most potent symbol of this attempt to market female assertiveness is the recent spate of ads which locate women as voyeurs and men as objects of sexual desire. In a 1995 ad for Sunburst orange juice, a line of men in tight orange shorts is checked out by two women in a gym. The girls lick their lips and make sexual squeezing gestures. The ad then dissolves into a fantasy sequence in which a pair of male buttocks turn into oranges.

The same year an ad for *Cleo* magazine showed two female researchers wandering along a line-up of naked men and apparently checking out their genitals. A voice-over narrated: 'The penis. It comes in all shapes and sizes. And in this month's *Cleo* we take a long, hard look at them'. Both ads attracted a barrage of complaints to the Advertising Standards Council. The aggrieved fell into three categories: those who felt the ads reinforced sexism against women by reinforcing the idea it's OK to objectify people; people who believe the ads constituted reverse sexism; and people who thought the ads were unacceptable on the grounds of taste and morality. A typical complaint stated the *Cleo* ad was sexist and 'would probably not have been allowed if it had shown naked women being measured by men' and 'is making fun of a subject that teenage men are particularly sensitive about'.

The chairman of the council responded by rejecting the reverse sexism argument. In his 1994 annual report he wrote: 'It has taken many years to achieve a generally fair representation in advertising, and this has come about only as the result of a major shift in community attitudes. Currently, what the community will accept in the way women are portrayed is very different from what is acceptable for men'. The council used this reasoning to dismiss complaints about the Sunburst orange juice ad. In its determination it stated that the community 'presently tolerates a higher degree of sexual assertiveness in women in relation to the opposite sex, than it does for men'.

Given the drubbing men have received for objectifying women, it's understandable some of them feel it's hypocritical to allow women to do the same to men. But the notion of reverse sexism misses the most important aspect of sexism—the role of male social and economic power. It's not the sexual objectification of women which feminism finds objectionable, but the idea that women are represented *solely* as objects of male desire. That they have been reduced to their usefulness to men. Women can objectify men without oppressing them because men are already seen as multidimensional human beings. Unfortunately, popular feminist debate encourages this reverse sexism argument by suggesting the real problem with sexual objectification is the way it 'dehumanises' people and degrades human sexuality. As I argue in chapter one, it's a position which the religious right and male opponents of feminism find all too easy to appropriate.

Arguing that gender equality lies in treating each other with unfailing quasi-religious 'respect' is winning feminism as many enthusiastic converts as banning women priests has won the Catholic Church. It's a utopian position which is totally out of touch with the diversity of contemporary sexuality. Ads about women drooling over cute boys have nothing to do with a return to the dark ages of patriarchy. When women turn men into objects, it's a sign they're exploring their own role as sexual *subjects*. They're finding out what it feels like to sit in the sexual driver's seat.

The recent deluge of articles on lesbian chic and bisexuality supports this theory. No longer labelled fat, ugly extremists, or more often simply ignored, the dyke community has been flung into the limelight. According to *Cleo*, *Esquire*, *Vanity Fair* and a host of popular magazines and newpapers, lesbians are suddenly sexy, savvy and stylish. *Time Out*'s special 'lover girls' issue summed up the trend when it asked readers: 'Lesbian culture is *the* 90s social phenomenon, but just how *au fait* are you with matters Sapphic? Can *you* tell your blazers from your leather brassieres?'. A guide to various members of 'the pussy posse' followed.

Perhaps more significantly the straight girl's bible, *Cleo*, ran a feature on lesbian chic which posed the following 'dilemma for the 90s woman'—if you could sleep with

Michael Hutchence or Helena Christensen, who would you choose? The readers responded in a survey published the following month—63 per cent plumped for Hutchence's girlfriend.

Girls in the dyke community who complain that the 'lesbian chic' trend misrepresents their diverse charms are missing the point. Articles on lesbian chic aren't necessarily about lesbians in the first place. More plausibly they're about nominally straight women and men and the reorganisation of gender politics attendant on the growing sexual and political assertiveness of women. Articles about lesbian chic, in other words, can act as a funnel for male anxieties about being made redundant and for female pleasure in testing newfound sexual power.

The nineties has also seen the resurgence of mainstream women's magazines aimed at women which incorporate pornography and erotica. In Australia, *Australian Women's Forum* mates centrefolds of naked, toned men with advice to women suggesting they forget diets 'because some fool with a size eight mind has designed ludicrously small bathing suits' and refuse 'to declare war on our gorgeous girlie girths'. *Forum* consistently inverts the traditional male-subject–female-object axis, actively promoting female voyeurism and sexual aggression. In doing so, it brings a feminist libertarian formula, which failed in the seventies when it was first (tamely) introduced via *Viva* and *Playgirl* back into the mainstream.

Some men, no doubt, find these public displays of sexual curiosity, assertiveness and even aggression on the part of women offensive and intimidating. It's probably not ameliorating the current angst about the meaning of masculinity any. But since when did a respectful attitude towards masculinity or the prescribed female role get women anywhere beyond the bedroom or the kitchen? And if some men feel humiliated by having the sexual gaze turned back on them, there are surely plenty who feel relieved and titillated to be able to relinquish some control.

DICK SCHTICK

I think lesbians do masculinity better than men do these days (lesbian interviewed in *Time Out*, June, 1995).

Quim magazine, a UK publication aimed at lesbians, carried an odd article in its fifth issue. The topic was gay–heterosexual sex—gay in the sense that all of the interviewees detailing their fantasies and practices consider themselves lesbian; heterosexual in the sense that the sex involved men. Some of their comments follow:

I want a big muscular leather man. Bushy mustache.

When I was a horny teenager I had a fantasy of fucking truck drivers with big rigs.

I get an urge sometimes for something hard that isn't detachable . . . Then I look at boys as a large sex toy which I can just use and throw away.

Boys for me are very emotional and not very sexual.

It's hardly a list of desires which most heterosexuals would instantly associate with lesbians—but then if you want to get a sense of just how labile the expression of contemporary gender and sexuality has become, lesbian magazines like Australia's *Wicked Women*, the UK's *Quim* and the North American *On Our Backs* are a good place to start.

Lisa Salmon, one of the founding editors of the Australian lesbian magazine *Wicked Women*, sums up the Zeitgeist when she says 'the seventies feminist thing just ended up being girls telling each other what to do. It became really dogmatic and it took the fun out of sexuality and being a dyke'. A performance artist and stripper, Salmon puts on a wig, lipstick and platform heels one day and butch trousers and Doc Martens the next. 'Dressing up to go out is a masquerade', she says. 'Girls will put on a moustache and go out as a boy one night or camp it up and go out as a girl. It extends into people's sex lives as well—just because a girl wears lipstick and long hair doesn't mean she's on the bottom between the sheets.' When she first entered the lesbian scene ten years ago, Salmon says she found the dress codes and attitudes to expressing sexuality oppressive. 'When I was 18, I went to a women's dance in my little mini dress and I looked around and saw Overall City—all these women in boiler suits and big boots. It was scary. Later on I started an S/M relationship and found that my girlfriend and I would get thrown out of dyke clubs for wearing fetish gear. We ended up in gay boys' bars where we were accepted.' (Lumby 1994e) As a result of their experiences, Salmon and her then girlfriend, Jasper Laybutt, started *Wicked Women*, a lesbian magazine featuring porn and S&M for women. They also began running an annual 'Ms Wicked' competition in which lesbians stripped and performed sexual acts for enthusiastic all-female audiences.

An insistent subtext of magazines like *Wicked Women* is

the notion that gender and sexuality are themselves a kind of drag performance—signs which can be played with in a pleasurable and defiant way. In the same way that gay men have turned the ultimate signs of straight masculinity—moustaches, muscles, construction-worker boots and crew cuts—into emblems of gay sexuality, lesbians are appropriating and reinventing traditional icons of heterosexuality—high heels and miniskirts, dildos and moustaches, and strip shows and lap dancing.

It's an attitude which characterises the nineties drag revival—a phenomenon which began in the queer community and quickly bubbled over into straight culture via movies like *Priscilla, Queen of the Desert* and drag performers like RuPaul. Cross-dressing for entertainment has a long history. Men routinely appeared in female parts in the public theatre of the English Renaissance and many of Shakespeare's most interesting roles involve plays on gender and appearance. In the twentieth century, plenty of mainstream performers have done drag, including Tony Curtis, Jack Lemmon, Dustin Hoffman, Milton Berle, Marlene Dietrich, Katharine Hepburn and Julie Andrews. But the nineties revival is a little different from traditional mainstream drag because of the way it openly challenges the traditional hierarchies of gender, sexuality and even race.

RuPaul is an African–American man who nudges seven feet in heels. He argues drag is all about reversing expectations. 'Why not just pump glamour to the hundreth degree? And why not have the most unlikely person of all do it—a big old black man?' In his autobiography, *Lettin' It All Hang Out*, RuPaul frequently sends up the expectations many women feel the fashion and advertising industries place on them. He describes his 'patented supermodel Tic Tac diet' in the following way: 'a Tic Tac for breakfast, a Tic Tac for lunch, and for dinner no Tic Tac—just a glass of water'. He comments: 'Naturally, I don't live by any of these guidelines—and neither should you. Instead, do as I do, which is to eat like a pig and then put on a strapping corset to suck it all in' (RuPaul 1995).

Feminists have often argued that drag is as insulting to women as Al Jolson's minstrel shows are to blacks. Discussing the drag revival in *New York* magazine Kim France argued that the underlying message of the average female impersonator 'is that drag queens not only make good women but make better women than real women, because they're willing to suffer more' (France 1995). France's objections are echoed by the feminists who derided Dustin Hoffman's cross-dressed performance in *Tootsie* as proof that even a man in a dress is taken more seriously as a professional than a real woman. But, as Marjorie Garber argues in her book on cross-dressing, *Vested Interests*, these criticisms fail to grasp the *in-betweenness* of drag. They look right through the transvestite to the man underneath. Drag queens, in other words, don't have to be seen as disguised men or fake women—they can be understood as a kind of third sex, as something which puts the traditional opposition of masculinity and femininity into question.

And if traditional femininity is now widely acknowledged as an exercise in pretending—a notion aptly summarised by Gloria Steinem's remark, 'I don't mind drag—women have been female impersonators for some time'—the strict dress and behaviour codes that define masculinity are rarely discussed. Drag may well be providing an opportunity to challenge these codes, along with the idea that men shouldn't experiment with femininity.

The popularity of the seventies retro soundtrack to *Priscilla, Queen of the Desert* suggests another dimension of contemporary drag—it's a sophisticated vehicle for processing pop cultural history, combining nostalgia, affection and satire in equal parts. RuPaul has described himself as 'a sampling machine . . . a collage made up of bits and pieces from old television shows, copies of *Vogue* magazine and advertisements'. Another New York drag performer, Jeff Roberson, also points out that when his generation of drag performers were growing up they didn't have big stars like Bette Davis and Joan Crawford to emulate. 'We grew up in the seventies, with bad TV shows like "Charlie's Angels"', he says. 'We had to create our own characters' (Busch 1995, p. 28). And in this sense modern drag channels and performs the destabilising impact popular culture has had on us all.

KEEPING THE MARGINS STRAIGHT

In an essay about having sex with gay men, United States lesbian feminist writer Pat Califia even suggests that the S/M scene exists beyond the traditional binaries of gender and sexuality altogether:

> I've thought a lot about why it's possible to cross the 'gender line' in the context of this kind of sex. First of all, in fisting [penetration with a fist] the emphasis is not on the genitals. Men at handballing [synonym for fisting] parties don't usually cruise each other's dicks. They cruise each other's hands and forearms. It is not

unusual for fisters to go all night without a hard-on (Califia 1994, p. 184).

An S/M practitioner, Califia prefers the tag 'sex radical' to lesbian. In her essay 'Gay Men, Lesbians and Sex: Doing It Together', from which the above quote is taken, she goes on to question the notion that a preference for certain sexual acts tells us anything about our identities. Gay men and lesbians, she suggests, 'have responded to persecution and homophobia by creating our own mythology about homo-sexuality'. Califia is less interested in what people do in bed than in their attitude to difference. A lesbian who condemns penetration is as 'straight' in her books as someone who does it in the missionary position every night.

Califia's observation about the way the signs of sex and sexuality are exchanged in contemporary culture points to a unexpected but real problem for marginalised groups: a fear of dissolving into the mainstream. After years of complain-ing about their 'invisibility', the lesbian community is dis-covering that media visibility comes with its own price tag, the chief cost being a loss of control over which images of lesbian identity circulate. Being 'out' also means allowing the straight community 'in' and with this intermixing comes a more diffuse, less essentialist notion of lesbian identity.

Debates in the Australian gay and lesbian community over whether to allow straight and bisexual people to join the Mardi Gras organisation and attend the annual Mardi Gras party are a classic instance of this anxiety. A festival which began life as a protest march, the Sydney Gay and Lesbian Mardi Gras illustrates the way the gay and lesbian community has, in one sense, become a victim of its own apparent acceptance. The desire, on the part of some in the lesbian and gay community, to exclude straight and bisexual people points up the role exclusion from mainstream society plays in founding a notion of community. Ironically, the accelerating representation of gays and lesbians in the press, on current affairs and talk shows, in television sitcoms and in Hollywood films, may do more to destabilise and fragment the lesbian and gay community than years of exclusion and hostility.

Feminists have to face a similar dilemma in the face of persistent mainstream media coverage. Exposure has opened feminism to competing representations of what it means to be a feminist. Despite persistent claims on the part of some feminists that the media continues to oppress women and ignore feminist views, the opposite is demonstrably true. As the 1994 battle for women viewers between *Real Life* and *A Current Affair* illustrated (see chapter six), stories on sex discrimination, sexual harassment, domestic violence and internal feminist debates are now regarded as highly saleable—even if these stories are done in a tabloid way. Books by feminists from Naomi Woolf to Helen Garner routinely become bestsellers. Newspapers run front-page stories about the heated public debate which results. The current problem for feminism is not oppressive patriarchal misrepresentations of women, but how to maintain a sense of identity in the face of a flood of competing images of feminism itself.

Five: Why feminists need porn

Cock, finger, toe, nipple, clit. Rewind. Cunt, butt, ear, mouth. Flip the page. Cock, finger, toe, nipple. Fast forward. Breast, arse, muscle, tongue. Pause. Every viewer or reader writes their own script when they look at pornography. No matter how explicit the material, no matter how beautiful the production values, no matter how perfectly a fantasy is reproduced, porn reminds us that desire always wants something more. A better viewpoint. A tighter close-up. A wider shot. Something off screen. A space between the frames.

Writing about pornography is absurd. Or, more precisely, pornography exposes the absurdity of the search for meaning at the heart of critical writing. Porn has no fixed narrative or truth. It turns us all into instant montage experts. Every video or magazine is a slippery stream of partial objects; a metonymic chain which mocks the earnest search for meaning as surely as it refuses us the perfect object of desire.

Most of us claim to know pornography when we see it. Common sense dictates that pornography is material produced for the purpose of arousing us sexually. As the Merriam Webster dictionary puts it, it's 'The depiction of erotic behaviour intended to cause sexual excitement'. Look a little closer though and the definition begins to seem hopelessly circular. So what's erotic? Something which 'tends to arouse sexual love or desire'. Which is? 'The depiction of erotic behaviour'.

The dictionary problem, of course, only reflects another commonplace about sexual responses and practices: one girl's hot slap and tickle is another boy's warm milk and Valium. Desire is elusive and subjective. It refuses to confine itself to particular acts, people, objects, imaginary sites or rooms in the house. Sexuality, as Elizabeth Grosz reminds us, 'is excessive, redundant, and superfluous in its languid and fervent overachieving. It always seeks more than it needs, performs excessive actions, and can draw any object, any fantasy, any number of subjects and combination of their organs into its circuits of pleasure' (Grosz 1994b, p. viii).

In a formal sense, debates about pornography have a lot in common with the practice of consuming pornography. Most discussions of pornography begin with a long-winded, feverish and ultimately futile search for a perfect definition or object. Pornography is not art, it's not erotica, it's not a love story, it's not real. The evil twin of a host of respectable cultural practices, pornography lies just out of reach, poised on the edge of a cultural fault line which is always threatening to erupt.

The controversy surrounding Elle Macpherson's decision to pose nude in US *Playboy* illustrates this need to police the boundaries between artistic nudity and porn. Macpherson walked around starkers for much of the film *Sirens* and revealed vast expanses of her flesh in her Bali calendar but no-one seemed to mind. It was her modest, playful *Playboy* shots which garnered public disapprobation. *Playboy* is porn, albeit soft core, the logic runs, and nice supermodels don't appear in magazines inclined to put staples through their navels.

This tenuous split between artistic nudity and porn echoes the framing of the nude in Western art. Supermodels, like fine-art nudes, are contemporary icons of Beauty, Taste and Ideal Form. Their toned, rapier-thin bodies, draped in surreally expensive clothes and jewellery, send out a clear message: look but don't touch. Porn models, on the other hand, symbolise the messy tactile world of sex. They're warm, fleshy and designed to look available.

Discussing this sacred split, art historian Lynda Nead argues that the female nude is a central ordering principle of art history and of cultural ideas about beauty and obscenity. The transformation of the ordinary unclothed female body into the high art female nude, she argues, is 'an act of regulation', both of the female body and of the viewer, whose responses are disciplined and directed by the conventions of art. In contrast, to the ordered and posed classical nude, Nead argues, pornographic images of women break this protective formal shield and show the disordered side of the female body—its orifices and fluids—which are both threatening and exciting to the viewer (Nead 1992).

In practice, the distinction between high art and pornography has never been easy to make. Ironically, Macpherson's appearance as a Norman Lindsay model in *Sirens* touches on exactly this problem—her nudity in the context of a film about an Australian artist is generally seen as more acceptable than her appearance in *Playboy* and yet, as the film makes clear, Lindsay's work is itself sexually exciting. The distinction between art and pornography is always a matter of framing. While Rubens' nudes may be arousing, the viewer's response to the images is supposedly contained by the context of the art gallery and by social constructions of art as uplifting and educative.

Asking 'what is pornographic?' is ultimately less productive than asking how and why a range of institutions and discourses, including feminism, have sought to define it. Pornography is inseparable from its use and regulation and from attempts to alternately discredit and valorise it. As the authors of a recent history of the policing of pornography note:

> . . . all attempts to provide a general statement of the truth of pornography—whether to discover its origin in the puritanical repression of healthy sexuality, its essence in the patriarchal objectification of women, or its rightful place in the sphere of private morality or in that of literary emancipation—must be greeted with a degree of scepticism (Hunter et al. 1993, p. viii).

Perhaps pornography can be most usefully understood as a blister—a tender spot on the social skin which marks a point of friction. Nothing, in these terms, is inherently, universally pornographic—the reference point for porn becomes an intersecting web of public policy, private desires and beliefs, and culture. In concrete terms, this disjuncture is arguably what gives pornography its charge— the fear and excitement it generates flows from the transgressions of real and imagined boundaries which traverse these categories. If we apply this definition broadly, there are arguably many forms of porn—there's food porn, fashion porn, home decoration porn, music porn. For some academics, watching commercial television counts as a form of pornography—it's something pleasurable and obsessive you do in private which involves trangressing boundaries you police publicly.

The idea that pornography has no essential character cuts against the grain of traditional feminist critiques of porn. Porn—the enemy—is supposed to be easy to spot. In the words of a famous feminist slogan coined by Robyn Morgan, 'pornography is the theory, and rape is the practice'. According to legislation drafted by antiporn activists Andrea Dworkin and Catharine MacKinnon, porn is a form of political speech which adds up to 'the sexually explicit subordination of women whether in pictures or in words' (Dworkin 1992, p. 525). To Australian feminist academic Sheila Jeffreys pornography is the 'propaganda of woman hatred', which 'teaches the second class status of women' (Deitz 1994).

The history of feminist debate seethes with women who claim they know porn when they see it and can anticipate the gruesome effects it produces in consumers. At the heart of contemporary feminist antipornography theory is a central belief: pornography is violence against women. As such it's the most literal and public illustration of endemic male fear and hatred of women. Pornography is held up as proof of a deep-rooted cultural misogyny. In this view of porn, it's a short step from the notion that pornography is a form of representational violence to the idea that pornography causes and perpetuates violence towards women in real life. And it's the latter argument which has been most important in mobilising the emotions, opinions and acts of resistance of feminists internationally.

PORN AND THE SWINGING VOTER

The debate about the effects of pornography on its viewers is confusing, inconsistent and complex. It roams across the fields of sociology, criminology, psychology, medicine, mass communications, art history, English literature, law andpublic policy, as well as feminism. Any conference organised around the theme of pornography is destined to include at least one heated exchange between authoritative study-wielding academics both hell-bent on discrediting the other's evidence. 'Definitive' conclusions in the field range from the 1986 United States Meese Commission Report, which appeared hopeful of holding pornography responsible for everything from herpes to lesbians, to Gore Vidal's wry observation that 'the only thing pornography is known to cause directly is the solitary act of masturbation' and its 'only immediate victim is English prose'.

The cause and effect debate has changed little in the way of opinions or policy. In the nebulous 'science' of quantifying social cause and effect there are inevitably more than enough studies to satisfy the needs of every interest group. As the past decade of debate about X-rated video material in Australia amply demonstrates, the quality of available research or academic argument usually has little bearing on what counts for 'evidence' when pornography meets the public sphere.

In 1984, an X rating for sexually explicit videos was first introduced in the Australian Capital Territory, following a 1983 agreement between state ministers and the federal attorney-general. Material initially classifiable under this rating was defined by the Film Censorship Board as material which included 'all depictions of sexual acts involving adults' but excepting 'those of an extremely sexually violent or cruel nature'. The guidelines were subsequently clarified and amended by the board to cover material which was 'sexually explicit but non-violent with no coercion of any kind'. X-rated videos came to designate only sexually explicit material—videos containing any hints of violence or coercion remained unclassifiable and illegal. This was supposed to be model legislation for the states.

Regardless, antiporn activists, including feminists, immediately began lobbying state attorneys-general and premiers to ban videos classified under the new X rating. In 1984, the conservative British antiporn activist, Mary Whitehouse, toured Australia with the Reverend Fred Nile and lobbied state premiers and ministers to ban material classified under the new rating. In a speech to the National Press Club in 1984, Ms Whitehouse continually invoked the generic scare term video 'nasty' without ever clarifying its relationship to the new legislation. She spoke instead of material which 'both sickened and distressed' those who saw it. She talked of 'disembowelling', of 'dismemberment' and 'decapitations', and continually returned to a familiar theme of antiporn conservatives: the dangerous impact of such material on the developing minds of the young. Her conflation of sex and violence was to become a familiar theme in the irrational debate which ensued over X-rated videos in Australia. Ms Whitehouse's obsession with protecting children and upholding the nuclear family at all costs is not surprising given that she's a traditional conservative. More surprising is the number of feminists and liberals who bought into the ensuing moral panic.

The term video 'nasty' neatly encapsulates the spectres which continue to dominate the feminist antiporn debate: child pornography and images of women being tortured, maimed and dismembered. In New South Wales, the Women's Advisory Council which advised then Premier Neville Wran on policy affecting women, condemned the introduction of the X rating. The stated view of the 12-member female board was that not only should sexually violent material be prohibited but that any material which 'shows sexually explicit subordination of women . . . including showing women as things, commodities or objects' should remain illegal. Wran responded quickly, choosing International Women's Day to announce that the whole issue of X-rated pornography would be re-examined. 'There are certain things', he said, 'that are beyond the pale'. He mentioned pack-rape, sado-masochism, and extreme violence in association with sex acts (Horin 1984 p. 12).

The fact that the X classification specifically excluded these images and was aimed only at enabling the rental or purchase of videos showing explicit and consensual sex between adults was buried under the ensuing outrage over explicit violence to women. Appeals were continually made to the decency of ordinary Australians, who (regardless of their news and current affairs diet) presumably don't want to see human beings maimed for real while they settled in with a video on Saturday night. The views of these 'ordinary' Australians were never sought on the real issue: the production and consumption of explicit images of consensual sex between adults.

In fact, national surveys conducted since the early 1980s consistently show overwhelming support for making sexually explicit, non-violent videos available to adults. A survey commissioned by the Office of Film and Literature Classification in 1992, for instance, found 70 per cent support for making X-rated videos available. This consistently high level of community support for making non-violent porn available has given the sex industry's main lobby group, the Eros Foundation, a solid base on which to build its campaign. In 1995, the *Good Weekend* magazine ran an article analysing the potential political power of the X-rated video-viewer vote. The author, Canberra press gallery journalist David Barnett, concluded that 'enough Australians watch X-rated videos in the 40 most marginal seats to decide the next election' (Barnett 1995, p. 53).

Barnett's claim may seem bizarre at first glance but an objective look at the industry's demographics supports his claim that the Eros Foundation has real political muscle. Despite being banned in all Australian states, X-rated videos are doing a roaring national trade. Almost a quarter of all films classified annually by the Office of Film and Literature Classification are X-rated and the industry is now turning over $20 million a year. As Robert Swan, a lobbyist for the sex industry, is fond of reminding politicians, the sex industry's mailing list is the second largest in the country. Almost three quarters of a million voting-age Australians buy X-rated videos by mail order and another 85 000 buy directly at shops in the ACT and Northern Territory. When the pass-on viewing rate is added (many consumers watch the movies they buy with their partners or friends), the Eros Foundation claims that more than a million Australians routinely view porn movies. That's around 7.5 per cent of the population.

Industry surveys both in Australia and the United States have consistently found that women and heterosexual couples (particularly women and couples under 40) make up a significant percentage of X-rated video purchasers and viewers. In the United States, where explicit sexual material is available from the local video store in many states, women make up 40 per cent of the adult video rental market. In Australia, a 1989 Australian Capital Territory survey of mail-order purchases of video porn showed that 30 per cent of people ordering videos were women. In-house surveys by Australian X-rated video stores also consistently indicate that well over half their renters are heterosexual couples.

Pornography is not the lonely province of desperate and depraved heterosexual men. Women, gay men, lesbians and bisexual people consume it too. In the lesbian community, in Australia, Canada, Britain and the United States, magazines such as *On Our Backs*, *Wicked Women*, *Bad Attitude* and *Quim* have been publishing pornographic fiction and images since the mid-1980s.

Yet, the public face of feminist debate on porn continues to be dominated by two straw figures: the bruised, beaten and otherwise abused porn actress and the cynical, callous male viewer. The fact that legally available sexually explicit material (the stuff you can obtain at video stores in the United States or via mail order from the Australian Capital Territory and Northern Territory) simply can't be classified at all if it involves scenes of violence or coercion is rarely discussed.

Pointing out that straight women or lesbians consume pornography is not, of course, an adequate reply to feminist claims that pornography constitutes representational violence against women. But it does serve to highlight an unpalatable and often hidden aspect of antiporn feminism. Faced with hard evidence that women are making up an ever greater percentage of the audience for pornography, proponents of censorship are forced to reveal the paternalistic and authoritarian roots of their argument: the belief that women who consume pornography are self-hating dupes who don't know what's good for them. Or as Catharine MacKinnon once put it, 'If pornography is part of your sexuality, then you have no right to your sexuality' (Kaminer 1992). The real problem with this position is that it exchanges the authoritative patriarchal view of 'what's good' for all women, with a matriarchal feminist one.

FROM FREE SPEECH TO EQUAL OPPORTUNITY

Freedom of speech has always been regarded as a central ethical principle of the liberal democratic state. Yet, as many feminists have argued, the free speech argument for not censoring pornography ignores a fundamental issue: not all speech is equally valued. Speech is not in fact free—money, power and a penis have been the traditional passports to the public sphere.

In an article she wrote about the 'chilling effect' of popular culture, Jocelynne Scutt contended that the dominant debate about censorship is 'lacking in understanding, much less analysis, of class, racism, ethnophobia and sexist ideology'. Her key point is that some speech is never heard and that the notion of 'free' speech masks a series of assumptions about what kind of speakers matter and what kind of listeners they're speaking to. She writes:

Free speechers do not question how or why a determination was made that the manuscript be published at
all. They do not question the loaded nature of their
whole concept of free speech: that some speech is never
heard; that publishers publish certain books and not
others; that decisions are made daily by newspapers,
television stations and book publishers as to what will
and won't appear (Scutt 1991, p. 81).

A more sophisticated critique of the liberal position
would involve broadening the production of speech, not
censoring it—a position feminists such as Dale Spender
adopted when they campaigned for a women's press. What
neither of these views address, though, is the complex
relationship between speech and sexuality. And it's precisely
this relationship which Michel Foucault addresses in his now
famous refutation of the theory that sex has been repressed
in Western societies. In *The History of Sexuality* Foucault
writes: 'What is peculiar to modern societies, in fact, is not
that they consigned sex to a shadow existence, but that they
dedicated themselves to speaking about it ad infinitum,
while exploiting it as the secret' (Foucault 1979, p. 35).

The implications of Foucault's critique of liberal assumptions are wide ranging and can't be addressed in full here.
There are, however, two key points to note. Firstly,
Foucault's argument suggests that pornography is not simply
an effect of sexuality, but rather, is a means of actively
producing the concept of sexuality itself. Sexuality, for
Foucault, is not a timeless, universal expression of human
desire, rather, sexuality is actively produced by forms of
professional knowledge and institutions dedicated to speaking its truth.

Christian confession, according to Foucault's argument, is intimately linked to the emergence of pornography itself. The rules of the confessional box—the requirement that each sexual act and thought be brought to light, catalogued and examined—is a powerful tool for teaching the connection between knowledge of sex and erotic pleasure. In this view, pornography does not arise from the repression of sex but from the injunction to speak of it. Foucault's argument also has important implications for the self-important claim often made by liberals that speaking out about pornography and sexual desire constitutes a radical act.

Foucault's account of sexuality and Western knowledge reveals the deeply pleasurable nature of taking up the 'radical' position. The claim that speaking openly about pornography requires self-insight and courage, in other words, merely repeats a commonplace about the relationship of sex to truth—the idea that sex is a hidden secret to which we must continuously return to uncover the truth about ourselves.

In the 1970s, feminists began to explore Foucault's work and consider its usefulness for feminist theory—a subject Meaghan Morris considered in her landmark essay, 'The Pirate's Fiancée', published in 1979. The importance of Foucault's work for feminists, as I suggest in the introduction to this book, reaches well beyond his discussions of sexuality, to his general analysis of the relationship between power and knowledge. To put it as simply as possible, his work suggests that feminists need to ask what kind of investment they have in the social institutions and practices they oppose.

But at the same time Foucault's work was beginning to

circulate among feminists, another very different analysis of the meaning of pornography was also gaining a foothold. Catharine MacKinnon, a highly charismatic American feminist, was developing her theory that pornography is more than the expression of male hatred of women, it is actually the primary means of their subordination. She wrote: 'Gender is sexual. Pornography constitutes the meaning of that sexuality. Men treat women as who they see women as being. Pornography constructs who that is.' (MacKinnon 1987, p. 172) Pornography, for MacKinnon, is the chief means by which men secure their dominance over women. She sees sexuality as far more important in constructing male-female relations than any other divisions in religion, the law, the family and the labour force.

MacKinnon believes the relations between men and women are entirely and completely formed by heterosexuality. Heterosexuality is the beginning and end of gender—it's a universal category which crosses race, class and ethnic boundaries and separates the oppressors from the oppressed. It's a seductive theory which has earned MacKinnon international fame in academia and the mass media. But it's also one which profoundly illustrates the way a self-assured, radical thesis like MacKinnon's winds up reinforcing (and perhaps actually inventing) the very system and practices it wants to abolish. MacKinnon's theory of gender and sexuality places male heterosexual desire and pornography at the centre of social relations and, in doing so, it assigns them enormous power.

In her fine essay on MacKinnon, Wendy Brown observes that the antiporn campaigner's social theory of gender works to shore up and reassert a set of traditional relations between men and women which have actually been eroded by a wide range of political and economic reforms. MacKinnon, Brown argues, makes heterosexuality the 'past, present and eternal future of gender'. She freezes pornography into a rigid text in which men are always dominant and women are always submissive and she implicitly devalues any other forms of sexuality, including lesbian and gay sexualities. MacKinnon is so insistent on the completeness of male domination of women, in fact, that her theory perversely mirrors the most conservative patriarchal vision of male– female relations. (Brown 1995, p. 88)

Poststructuralist feminist critiques may have made mince-meat out of MacKinnon's theories, but her ideas have had a wide-ranging impact on popular ideas about pornography and gender in the mid-'80s and '90s. It is hardly surprising to see, looking back over this period, that MacKinnon's views have been used across the globe to fuel an alliance between conservatives and feminists.

The farcical 1986 United States Meese Commission hearings into 'and subsequent report on' pornography were a touchstone in this regard. Stacked with conservatives and moral crusaders, the commission took its cue from an assumption voiced at the outset of the inquiry by US Attorney-General Edwin Meese that 'the content of pornography has radically changed, with more and more emphasis upon extreme violence'. The commission held public hearings addressed by numerous feminist witnesses who gave emotive testimony about their experience as 'victims' of pornography. The final report, which endorsed the Dworkin and MacKinnon view that pornography constitutes a violation of women's civil rights, was hailed as a victory for feminism. The fact that the moral panic feeding the Meese Commission's deliberations flowed from the same wellspring which threatened abortion rights, sex education programs, the availability of cheap contraception, gay and lesbian rights and the Equal Rights Amendment for women was strangely lost on antiporn advocates.

In Canada, Dworkin- and MacKinnon-style feminism has had even greater success. In 1992, the Canadian Supreme Court issued the Butler decision which replaced the traditional community standards test of obscenity with one drawn, in part, from a brief submitted by Catharine MacKinnon. The decision has resulted in a flurry of activity by Canadian customs officials often aimed at gay, lesbian and feminist material. Black feminist academic bell hooks, lesbian feminist writer Pat Califia, fiction writer Kathy Acker and even Andrea Dworkin herself are just a few of the authors whose works have been seized. Summing up the impact of the Butler decision, Nadine Strossen writes:

> Within the first two and a half years after the Butler decision, well over half of all Canadian feminist bookstores had materials confiscated or detained by customs. From Quebec to Victoria, Canadian bookstore managers had the same comment: that Butler increased censorship in Canada by customs, police and the lower courts, and that the predominant targets have been gay, lesbian and women's literature (Strossen 1995, p. 231).

In Australia, similar rhetoric has fuelled a host of parliamentary inquiries and reports. In 1992, then Victorian Premier Joan Kirner used a conference on the status of women to call on attorneys-general and censorship ministers to develop guidelines on the classification of print and video material that dealt with three major issues: 'material which condones or incites violence against women, material which shows women in demeaning sexual poses, and banner advertising of restricted magazines'. The ease with which Kirner's recommendation glosses over the extremely contentious question of what 'demeaning sexual poses' look like and conflates such images with sexism and violence illustrates the extent to which antiporn feminist views have become naturalised.

Antiporn feminists have also recently sought to bring the harm they claim is done by pornography under the banner of sex discrimination. It's an astute political shift for two reasons: firstly, it buys out of the age-old, circular liberal debate about balancing freedom of speech with community standards and secondly, it buys into a wealth of existing, efficient and respected laws and institutions set up to deal with discrimination against women. The potential harm of pornography has often been understood in terms of the harm it might cause men to do—rape women or otherwise abuse them. But the pornography-as-discrimination argument takes the focus off what pornography supposedly causes men to do and puts it onto what pornography supposedly does to women, which is to sexually subordinate them.

The difference between the liberal notion of harm and the feminist argument about discrimination may seem like sophistry. But its impact on public policy is potentially enormous. To give a striking example, the feminist equation: porn=sex discrimination opens the way for legislation enabling women to sue their male partners for leaving *Penthouse* magazine lying around at home.

Catharine MacKinnon is often credited with pioneering the idea that sexual harassment is a form of sex discrimination. It's a notion which the United States courts have widely accepted. It follows, then, that if MacKinnon and her supporters are successful in getting courts and/or parliaments to define the harm of pornography as a form of sex discrimination, existing laws concerning sexual harassment can be used by antiporn feminists to attack people who consume pornography in the workplace and, if some feminists have their way, at home.

Nadine Strossen comments on the United States situation:

> . . . the Supreme Court has unanimously accepted the argument that sexual harassment is gender-based discrimination. Therefore, when employers, campus officials, judges, and other policy makers accept the argument that pornography, in turn, *is* sexual harassment—as many distressingly have done—then, in effect, they have accepted the claim that pornography is gender-based discrimination (Strossen 1995).

This manoeuvre, Strossen concludes, comprises a strategic backdoor way for the pro-censorship feminist camp to enshrine their views in law. And, as Moira Gatens argues in her book on gender politics and ethics, *Imaginary Bodies*, there's a real danger that legislating this view of male and female sexuality will actually give it reality. She writes:

> Both Catharine MacKinnon and Andrea Dworkin propose essentialised conceptions of male/female sexualities

that, if encoded in the law, will entrench conservative and destructive active/passive notions of male and female embodiment. As Michel Foucault has convincingly shown, the legal and medical regulation of human behaviour tends to produce subjects who 'recognise' themselves in these regulative discourses (Gatens 1996, p. 78).

THE BIGGEST FANTASY OF ALL

For the Australian feminists who demanded that an issue of the magazine *People* be relegated to porn shops on account of its cover, a photo of a naked woman in a dog's collar exemplifies misogyny. For lesbian feminist writer and S/M aficionado Pat Califia, the sight of a woman in a collar (or handcuffs and gags) is a turn-on.

Califia is an intellectually able and witty commentator on the politically slippery territory of her own sexuality. She has written widely, critiquing both the feminist antipornography movement and the desire of some lesbians and gays to deny a voice to members of their communities who indulge in S/M. But to many antiporn feminists, Califia's sexual preferences are the ultimate expression of how deeply our culture has embedded sexist power relations—even self-proclaimed lesbian feminists perpetuate them.

Australian academic and lesbian feminist writer, Sheila Jeffreys illustrates a common response to Califia's interest in S/M and porn:

The models we are offered of female sexuality are of passivity and submission . . . Where we live under oppression and where there is virtually no escape for us, at least until we reach an advanced age, toward egalitarian relationships in which we take sexual initiatives, we have little alternative but to take pleasure from our oppression. The most common response is to eroticise our powerlessness in masochism (Jeffreys 1993, p. 179).

Califia responds:

I am interested in something ephemeral—pleasure—not in economic control or forced reproduction. This may be why S/M is so threatening to the established order and why it is so heavily penalised and persecuted . . . Our political system cannot digest the concept of power not connected to privilege (Califia 1994, p. 163).

Many feminists amenable to Califia's analysis of S/M practice and its pleasures will be quick to point out that it's a long step from a fantasy acted out between two consenting lesbians and an image adorning the cover of a magazine bought primarily by men. Or is it? In fact, Califia's argument sheds as much light on the latter scenario as the former. Context and category, she reminds us, are everything when it comes to both sex and sexism. Appearance is mobile—something producers of a magazine like *People* are perfectly aware of. The magazine is a self-conscious, crass spoof of male desire, albeit one which simultaneously feeds the desires it mocks. Satire is only one of the intangibles which evaporate when the image of a woman in a dog-collar is reduced to its literal elements.

It's an account of image production and consumption which antiporn feminists cannot afford to accept. Because at the heart of their argument against pornography is a belief that truth is always contaminated and distorted by images. Catharine MacKinnon exemplifies this belief when she writes: '. . . sex in life is no less mediated than it is in art. One could say men have sex with their image of a woman. It is not that life and art imitate each other; in this sexuality, they are each other' (1992, p. 463).

The implication of MacKinnon's critique is that in a truly equal world, a world without sexual politics, men and women would relate in an unmediated way—'false' images would not intrude on 'real' human relations. There would be sexuality without objectification. The pure truth behind appearances will out. Speaking at a 1993 conference on sex and censorship, spokesperson for the Coalition Against Sexual Violence Propaganda, Liz Conor, exemplified this desire when she said she had nothing against sexually explicit material, as long as it was devoid of 'sexual politics'.

This dream of pure presence is deeply rooted in Western metaphysics, in an opposition between truth and its representation which goes back to Plato. According to this tradition, representations or signs, begin by standing in for the truth but wind up corrupting and distorting it. Truth, like God, always precedes its representation.

Antiporn feminists argue that women's true sexual selves exist somewhere outside their manipulation by male desire, that women have been silenced—literally, gagged—by the false images purveyed by pornographers. Pornography, in this scenario, is no less than the obliteration and rewriting of women's very being.

Yet, even if we accept this argument and take it to its logical conclusion we still find ourselves right back where we started—at the problem of representation. If all images have a tendency to mask and distort the truth about human relations, then where do antiporn feminists draw the line? Where does pornography stop and erotica begin? How could we represent 'unmediated' sexual relations? The brave new world proposed by MacKinnon and Dworkin is at the end of the day, a very old and familiar utopia: the dream of a place outside representation, outside language, beyond communication, a place without self and other, a zone of pure presence.

There is, of course, nothing wrong with fantasising. Indeed, in a formal sense, the feminist debate on pornography might be understood as a fantasy in the pornographic sense. There's an obsessive and deeply pleasurable return to the same old issues. The debates are often highly charged and the same artificial schism reinvents itself: the Good Girls who exhibit fear and repulsion about pornography and the Bad Girls who get a kick out of being politically out of line. Not that there's anything particularly wrong with the feminist obsession with porn. On the contrary, obsessions tell us where the friction is and hopefully lead us to ask relevant questions about historical and contemporary causes.

Fantasy is about wish fulfilment—wishes which are not always consciously recognised and which may not represent anything we would necessarily do if we had the time or the opportunity. In fantasy, contradictory impulses and impossible coalitions of subjects and objects coexist quite happily. Pornography is sometimes a funnel for this kind of wish fulfilment. In a similar sense, the feminist debate about pornography is also a kind of fantasy. It's a meeting point for the desires of different feminists—a forum for articulating what we want feminism to be. In this light, the notion that you can draw a cause and effect line between fantasy and social practice is disturbing and distasteful to some feminists. It denies a different kind of desire for feminism—one which grounds feminism in political strategy and argues for the need to continually question its own relationship to other ideas and institutions.

Six: The news without underpants

Breast implant addicts. On-camera liposuction. Charles and Camilla's secret love-tapes. Teenage lesbian vampires. Date rape. Miracle cancer cures. Bisexual kindergarten teachers. Surfing rabbits. Cellulite. Latex. Gutter journalism. Mass crass. Trash TV. Or as one Australian tabloid dubbed it—'the news without underpants'. It's here. We leer. But media critics don't seem to be getting used to it.

In the past decade, every conceivable media format, from prime-time news bulletins and current affairs programs to traditional women's magazines seems to have developed a taste for the tabloid. It's a trend which has sparked heated debate in Australia and the United States. Critics across the political spectrum argue the tabloid invasion is responsible for everything from voter apathy to family breakdown.

Behind many of these criticisms is an elitist and authoritarian view of what issues matter and what the public ought to be interested in. It's a view rooted in a traditional, paternalistic conception of the public sphere which privileges the world of business, parliamentary politics, medical science, law, economics and tertiary education, while relegating the personal and social extensions of these institutions and disciplines to the domestic sphere. It's the kind of double-think which has allowed domestic violence to be seen as a private matter between husband and wife, while a fight between mates in a pub is treated as a criminal matter.

The tabloid trend has put 'private' issues on the nightly televisual map, from domestic violence and child abuse, to relationships, addiction, eating disorders, parenting problems and sexuality. It blurs the boundaries between women's stuff and traditional public policy matters. And by juxtaposing the usual serious news fare with the tabloid—putting the public health problem of drug abuse up against personal battles with addiction, for instance—it connects the public and private spheres in an intuitive way that feminists have long agitated for at the public policy level. In this chapter I want to explore the positive implications of this tabloid trend in our media and look at the role of the public sphere in a postmodern world.

DISCOVERING THE FEMALE VIEWER

Close your eyes and picture this surreal scenario. It's 6.00 p.m. on a Wednesday night in a suburban Sydney home. A key turns in the front door, the dog starts barking and all the kids race down the hall. Dad's home from work. Mum, who's in the kitchen putting the final touches to dinner, straightens her skirt and hurriedly reapplies her lipstick. But before anyone can bother him with mundane chitchat, the head of the household has something more important to do. It's news time—and Dad wants to catch up on the world's events in peace and quiet. He settles down in his armchair with a sherry and the rest of the family tiptoes around him for half an hour.

In 1960s Australia, men worked and their wives frequently stayed at home. In 1961, around 20 per cent of women were in paid employment. By 1991, two-thirds of married women in the peak working years between 25–54 were in the labour force and studies show that most of the remaining one-third will have worked at some time during marriage. (McDonald 1995) Daytime television catered to women and children with soap operas, chat shows and cartoons. Evening television was a man's domain of news and current affairs shows. Wives watched what their husbands watched. Today, it would be a brave man who told his wife or girlfriend to let him watch the news in peace and go get his dinner ready. With the bulk of Australian women aged 25–54 now in the full-time workforce, the genders are equal consumers of prime-time television. In fact, women viewers now consistently dominate the early evening news and current affairs slots in Australia.

Some senior production executives at the Australian networks have been slow to grasp this shift, and often literal-minded in their bid for female viewers. The 'women viewer' issue came to a head in 1993 when Channel Seven launched a new current affairs program, 'Real Life'. Fronted by the softly spoken Stan Grant, it was promoted as a program specifically designed to appeal to women as well as men. Executive producer Gerald Stone, who also worked as executive producer on Channel Nine's '60 Minutes' and 'A Current Affair', was largely responsible for that focus. He recalls what motivated him:

In my years at '60 Minutes', I was aware of the power of the family audience but it was also clear to me that sometimes we'd get a strongly pro or adverse reaction to a story and it was the woman's hand which was changing the dial. Then I went away to the States for a few years and when I came back and looked at Channel Nine in an objective way it was obviously a very macho channel. Even though 'A Current Affair' had Jana Wendt it was still a very macho thing—Jana was doing very aggressive interviews, they did ambushes and they were chasing villains down the street. So I said, 'Well, it seems like all they're doing is boy's own reporting' (Lumby 1994a).

In response, Stone said he made sure reporters on 'Real Life' went out of their way to identify and report on issues he believed women want to know more about—at what Stone described as the 'heavy' end of the current affairs spectrum. That meant dealing with issues like sexual harassment, sex discrimination in the workplace, eating disorders and domestic violence. At the lighter end, 'Real Life' also concentrated on the type of stories covered by many women's magazines—dieting, grooming, fashion and women's health issues.

In the program's first year the formula was apparently a huge hit. Women viewers flocked to 'Real Life', which began beating 'A Current Affair' in ratings in mid-1993. It was the first time the long-running Channel Nine program had been knocked off its perch by a rival current affairs program. Channel Nine was worried, and rightly so. The power of the female viewer amounts to more than simple ratings. Market research consistently shows that women are the principal household shoppers, so they are also the primary target group for many advertisers. They are not only likely to notice advertisements for traditional women's products like cosmetics, perfume or household goods, they are far more likely than men to notice ads for men's wear, electrical items and furniture. When women viewers switch channels, millions of advertising dollars switch with them.

Channel Nine was quick to respond. In 1994, 'A Current Affair' dumped the more macho Mikes—Munro and Willesee—in favour of Ray Martin, a presenter who had established his track record with a female audience on a successful midday talk show. And while the executive producer of 'A Current Affair', Neil Mooney, denied that the program was specifically targeting women, the old aggressive foot-in-the-door style of story went too.

In the United States, this tabloid trend in current affairs programming is even more pronounced. Three of the major networks—CBS, NBC and Fox—respectively run the tabloid current affairs programs 'Hard Copy', 'Inside Edition' and 'A Current Affair', in prime time five nights a week. And all three shows exhibit a radical departure from issues-based, analytic prime-time fare, in favour of a focus on private lives and personalities. Classic stories involve ordinary people caught up in extraordinary circumstances—sexually extroverted behaviour or violent crime being the favourite narratives—or extraordinary people (celebrities) trapped by the ordinary—romance, addiction, domestic violence and divorce. A 1994 'Hard Copy' episode, for instance, consisted of a story on Prince Charles' marriage breakdown, Oprah Winfrey's childhood traumas and the videotaped confession of a murderer. This fixation with private lives is underscored by the genre's love affair with hidden cameras and illicit amateur video footage—the 'sex, lies and videotape' stories which frequently feature an 'ordinary' suburban couple engaging in 'extraordinary' sexual behaviour.

The immense popularity of these formats suggests feminists need to think carefully before they make sweeping claims about what women viewers want or what they ought to want (claims I discuss below). Male television producers are not the only ones who are capable of patronising women or ignoring their needs. Feminists are in danger of doing exactly the same thing when they portray consumers of tabloid television as powerless dupes.

The male prime time/female daytime dichotomy has crumbled. The majority of women aged 25–54 now work full time and, therefore, watch television (or listen to it) in the evening. The excesses of emotion, gossip and human interest once relegated to soap operas and daytime chat shows now dominate our current affairs programs and much of our news. Tabloid television's conflation of the public and private spheres only highlights a tendency already inherent in global mass-media culture.

TALKING BACK

In 1995, United States senators Sam Nunn and Joe Lieberman joined forces with former US Secretary of Education William Bennett to rid the United States of the 'cultural rot' at the heart of daytime talk shows. Senator Lieberman, a Democrat, told a press conference that: 'Talk is indeed cheap and too often on these shows it is also demeaning, exploitative, perverted, divisive and immoral'. Their advocacy group, Empower America (ironically, a name which echoes talk-show therapy jargon), pressured advertisers to boycott programs the group found morally offensive (Mifflin 1995, p. 22).

At the heart of criticisms of the talk shows is the notion that they take issues which decent and rational people normally keep private and make them public, and that they rely on the gullibility and bad judgement of their working-class guests to do so. A *New York Times* article analysed the 'cynical business' of finding talk-show guests and concluded: 'Under the guise of exploring emotional issues, the shows are really looking for stories that will entertain and produce high ratings. And producers acknowledge that the people willing to appear on these shows are disproportionately poor and uneducated' (Kolbert 1995, p. 2). The underlying assumption is that there's something universally undignified and inherently damaging about confessing your problems to a national audience.

But 'poor' and 'uneducated' people may not find middle-class views about what should be properly public or private either pragmatic or pleasurable. Instead of condemning talk-show guests for their tasteless behaviour, why not view talk shows as a democratic extension of the psychotherapist's couch (home to the *wealthy* worried well) or a secular version of the confessional? Like the box and the couch, talk shows are not simply about solving people's problems—they're about the *process* of sharing them around. To put it another way, even expensive professional psychoanalysis is not all *analysis*—a lot of it involves plain talking.

It's also worth remembering that television plays a significant and varied role in the lives of many people—one which books, e-mail and cinema may fill for middle-class journalists or academics. The idea that television is an inappropriately superficial medium for examining social problems or that there's something 'sad' about people who gain a sense of intimacy and shared experience from a television program is bound up with a rigid and elitist view of what constitutes a 'proper' forum. The idea that the only appropriate way to deal with personal problems is in a rational one-to-one conversation with a professional or objective third party may not be particularly useful or practical for a woman who's bringing up three children on welfare.

On a more fundamental level, the idea that talk shows are messing up the public sphere with trivial gossip buys into some very old gender stereotypes about what we should talk about and how we should say it. Women's conversation has traditionally been slighted as trivial, irrational, emotional, confessional and immoderate. When men talk they're supposedly analytical, objective, restrained and economical. At least, that's the myth. But, as even a brief listen to conservative United States and Australian commercial talk-back radio programs makes clear, there is nothing inherently female about talk media. Right-wing male talk-show hosts might tout themselves as political cowboys who are reclaiming the public sphere from 'soft' liberal, feminising influences, but if you look behind the superficial masculinity of their style—the polemic, abrasive, take-no-prisoners rhetoric—it becomes very clear that they're every bit as passionate, personal and locquacious as a guest on a talk show.

But you don't need to go to the right-wing pressure valves of contemporary media for evidence that the pejorative labelling of talk shows as socially corrupt feminine nattering is a touch selective. The cradle of quality journalism itself, the seventeenth century public sphere, was basically built on idle chatter. Early magazines, such as *Tatler* and *Spectator*, grew out of the seventeenth century coffee houses and their salon-like atmosphere. They provide enduring evidence that even in the Enlightenment, caffeine-fuelled conversation didn't simply dwell on metaphysics and science, but often turned to juicier subjects.

In many senses, the news as we understand it today is simply a refined form of gossip. Journalists track down stories, frequently using anonymous sources who they can trade information and influence with. Often the only real difference between so-called quality news and tabloid reports is the value given to the subject matter according to a masculine, public sphere/feminine, private sphere split. It's the kind of logic which says a story about surviving factional party politics is hard news but a story about negotiating common family arguments is trivial.

TAKING OUT THE TRASH

In 1989, the American Broadcasting Corporation correspondent Jeff Greenfield epitomised popular concerns about tabloid television when he spoke out against a trend which 'seemed to threaten the American way of life, even the American family' in the form of 'tabloid TV, trash TV—the new nonfiction television programs that feature murders, celebrity break-ups, and sex scandals'. Comparing television's decline to the person who could not resist thumbing through a *Penthouse* magazine at the airport, Greenfield argued tabloid entertainment values were 'all id and no superego—the carriers of the basest impulses, unrestrained by shame or, for that matter, pride' (Weiss 1989, p. 38). Former Watergate reporter Carl Bernstein backed up Greenfield's comments, when he decried 'the creation of a sleazoid infotainment culture in which the lines between Oprah and Phil and Geraldo and Diane and even Ted, between the *New York Post* and *Newsday*, are too often indistinguishable' (Bernstein 1992, p. 24). In Australia, media critic Stuart Littlemore has made similar criticisms of the tabloid trend in news and current affairs arguing that commercial current affairs programs are prostituting the ideals of the fourth estate.

Feminists have joined these critics, claiming tabloid television manipulates its female viewers and often cruelly exploits women. *Ms* magazine, for example, damned one of tabloid television's staples—the TV talk show—for presenting women 'as perpetual victims' with 'so little power that not only do they have to contend with real dangers such as sexual or physical abuse, but they are also overcome by bad hair, big thighs, and beautiful but predatory "other" women' (Heaton & Wilson 1995, p. 45).

Tabloid media is said to work like a drug—it hooks people and corrupts them. Sounding rather like a nineteenth-century pamphlet about masturbation, one critic wrote: 'Surely there ought to be a way the public could be weaned away . . . The short-term guilty pleasure we get from wallowing in prurience and sensationalism has the harmful, long-term effect of desensitising us, making us immune to outrage, so heavy is the air with outrageous acts'. A good start, he suggested, would be for the media to cut down on the space they devote each day to 'seamier acts' (Gelbart 1995, p. 42).

This picture of tabloid consumers as indulgent, passive, suggestible and easily distracted from more worthy intellectual pursuits echoes the stereotype of the female consumer. Women are symbolically tied to capitalism's most frequently deplored features: artifice and consumption. From the overweight couch potato who weeps over Meg Ryan's latest romantic comedy to the dazed bimbo who trashes her husband's credit card at the local mall, female consumers are supposed to be simultaneously too involved (too easily seduced) *and* too passive (incapable of discrimination). Men, on the other hand, are supposedly self-sufficient, productive and rational (implicitly difficult to influence with advertisements or glamorous packaging).

What's more, popular culture itself is often criticised for promoting qualities traditionally associated with women. Shopping, following fashion, wearing cosmetics, watching talk shows, reading glossy magazines—all these activities are derided for promoting vanity, excessive emotion and gratuitous spectacle. Just consuming them is a supposedly feminising process—'real' men can't shop or match their tie with their socks.

Lynne Joyrich sums up the origin of this gendering of mass culture and its consumption when she writes that 'in the popular imagination, the woman is too close to what she sees—she is so attached that she is driven to possess whatever meets her eye . . . Such everyday appraisals of women as subjects who lack the distance required for "proper" reasoning and viewing are mirrored by theoretical and psychoanalytic accounts of femininity which similarly stress women's lack of subject/object separation' (Joyrich 1990, p. 162). Women, in other words, are supposedly incapable of maintaining the proper distance between their true selves (their subjectivity) and the multiple images they present to the outside world (their status as objects). They're forever staring in the mirror or flipping through magazines to see who they are. But there are more optimistic and less moralistic ways to look at the relationship between gender and consumption.

The historical alignment of women and mass culture suggests women have a uniquely knowing relationship to consumer culture. They've been well trained in appreciating and managing the politics of appearances—a strength which feminist philosopher Luce Irigaray has explored. Irigaray argues that women shouldn't emulate the male quest for self-containment and objective truth but rather embrace the ambiguity and flexibility of masks or appearances (Irigaray 1985). It's a very different philosophy of the self to the dominant Western tradition which values self-mastery and stable identity. But it's one which suggests creative new ways in which feminists can rethink the symbolic relationship between femininity and consumption.

BEYOND THE PUBLIC SPHERE

It's often claimed that the contemporary tabloid trend in television, newspapers and magazines is corrupting journalism's role as a facilitator of rational public debate. In this scenario, quality journalism is supposed to have a dual role: providing a forum for public opinion, as well as acting as a watchdog over institutions like our courts, our legal system and our parliament. But whether it's emanating from outside commentators or professional journalists themselves, public debate is ideally meant to be dispassionate, analytic and information driven.

The ideals of open, rational and critical debate spawned in the Enlightenment are central to modern formulations of quality journalism's role in the public sphere and, by extension, democracy. The best-known theorist of the public sphere is the German social theorist, Jurgen Habermas, who argues that the modern public sphere—and its corollary, public opinion—has its genesis in a whole range of cultural institutions, from coffee houses and literary salons, to opera houses, lecture halls, theatres, libraries and the commercial presses (Habermas 1989). In its simplest terms, the modern, post-Enlightenment public sphere is a forum where public opinion can be developed and exchanged on issues affecting commerce and the state. A particularly important feature of the modern public sphere, from Habermas's point of view, is the idea that it allowed private citizens to come together as equals and debate issues and ideas in a reasonable manner.

Habermas saw the public sphere as a foundation of modern democracy. But in recent years, a number of writers have discussed the way the public sphere has historically excluded people on the base of race, religion, class and gender. In feminist terms, the public sphere has traditionally marked the limits of the recognition of women's economic, intellectual and social role.

Habermas acknowledges that women have been traditionally excluded from the political public sphere, but he sees this as part of the limitations of existing society not of his model of a universal public in which pre-existing inequalities between individuals can be bracketed off to permit equal and reasoned discussion. Rejecting this claim, Moira Gatens argues that the very idea and structure of the modern public sphere relies on the exclusion of women and all things associated with them. The private sphere, in other words, is the necessary, invisible foundation of the public sphere. She writes: 'The world of the family, infant education, morality and sensuality is private, domestic, whereas the world of work, citizenship, legality and rationality is public. Man's possibilities are predicated on women remaining static' (Gatens 1993, p. 12).

Two centuries after the Enlightenment, the same terms continue to underpin discussions of the contemporary media's role in the public sphere. The family, the body, sexuality and relationship issues are relegated to the 'natural' 'feminised' private sphere while political and economic interests are located in the 'cultural' 'masculine', public domain. What's more this opposition provides self-justifying grounds for the ongoing exclusion of everything aligned with the feminine from the public sphere. 'Woman is constructed as close to nature, subject to passion and disorder, and so excluded from the rational body politic, which then constructs her as its enemy, or as Hegel phrases it, as its "everlasting irony"' (Gatens 1993, p. 97).

Seen in this light, much of the debate about the contamination of traditional news values by the irrational, indecently personal focus of tabloid journalism emerges as a desire to police the boundaries of a symbolic masculine space. On closer examination many of the 'improper' themes of tabloid television look like public-sphere issues seen through the looking glass. Take the different way the human body is framed in 'quality' as opposed to tabloid journalism. In traditional news broadcasts, the body tends to arise as either an object of expert knowledge (as something to be enhanced, cured or otherwise regulated by scientists, sports physiologists or doctors) or as one of institutional control (as an addicted or aberrant body which needs guidance from public health officials). On tabloid television, however, the body as object of expert study is exchanged for the lived body as most of us experience it in our everyday life. 'Ordinary' people are interviewed about being overweight, smoking or drinking too much, or failing to get an erection—their day-to-day experience effectively qualifying them to be their own 'experts'. In the tabloid media, in other words, the body is shown to be more than a logical network of biological parts or statistically verifiable behaviours—it's also an extension and motivator of unpredictable human needs and wants.

In the same way that it substitutes 'average' people for experts, the tabloid media also frequently spurns traditional forms of knowledge—medicine, science and economics—for their irrational, populist counterparts—faith-healing, astrology and psychics. In this sense, tabloid journalism can be seen as a route for the return of everything the traditional public sphere sought to repress—emotion, superstition, desire, fantasy, gossip, the irrational. At the same time, it also uncovers hidden continuities between the public and private spheres.

The tabloid media coverage of the murder trial of American football hero O.J. Simpson is a case in point. Critics of the enormous tabloid media interest in the trial frequently decried the relentless focus on the private lives of the public personalities involved in the trial—in particular, the defendant, witnesses and counsel—for obscuring the key legal issues in the case. But the two major issues raised by the case—the domestic violence O.J. Simpson allegedly subjected his wife to and the institutional racism of the Los Angeles police—are both pervasive social problems which have been allowed to fester precisely because of this demand that the public and private spheres be kept separate. Domestic violence has traditionally been treated as a personal matter between husband and wife, while the fiction that everyone is equal before law has allowed the prejudicial effect of everyday racism to go unacknowledged by courts.

The tabloid media's tendency to blur the lines between the public and private spheres is not just a matter of content, however. Tabloid coverage and televising of the O.J. trial also established a continuity between the courtroom and the lounge room. The performance of counsel, traditionally reserved for the benefit of the judge and jury, was mapped onto a televisual performance, showing that the courtroom, just as much as tabloid television, is an arena of performance, emotion and spectacle. And unlike classical journalism, which directs anxiety outward toward the forces which threaten its boundaries, tabloid television incorporates this anxiety about the relationship between the public and private into its format and focus.

ENTERTAINMENT AS CULTURE

In 1989, former United States President Richard Nixon gave President-elect George Bush the benefit of his thinking on television news. Writing in *TV Guide* he told Bush that television is 'an entertainment medium, not an educational one' and that on television 'being interesting is infinitely more important than being responsible' (Nixon 1989).

The formal properties of print and television certainly lend themselves to starkly different news cultures. Television news favours discrete clumps of information over extended argument or analysis. It also foregrounds the expressive content of a message—the private emotional cues which are lacking in the public content of a direct printed quote. As a medium which requires images, television feeds off attractive individuals and personalities. Abstract, discursive debate is not regarded as popular television. Lively, expressive people, regardless of the quality of their ideas, are. Debates about news and current affairs journalism often minimise these differences in favour of establishing a continuity between broadsheet print reporting and 'serious' news and current affairs journalism. Yet, it's a formula which locates television within a print-oriented hierarchy and ignores the distinctive characteristics of the electronic mass media and the social and institutional relations it engenders.

As cultural theorist John Thompson notes, it's also a formulation of the media's role in the public sphere which obliges us to interpret the growing role of electronic media as a historic fall from grace. He proposes instead that we should 'recognise from the outset that the development of communication media . . . has created a new kind of publicness which cannot be accommodated within the traditional model' (Thompson, 1994, p. 98).

In *No Sense of Place* Joshua Meyrowitz argues that television assaults the dividing line between male and female worlds because 'it merges traditionally distinct gender information systems, blurs the dividing line between the public and private behaviours of each sex and undermines the significance of physical segregation as a determinant of sex segregation'. Television, he claims, helped break down the domestic isolation of many women in the fifties and sixties by offering them a direct window onto the world of the public male sphere. In this scenario, content (what women were told their place was by television programmers) is less important than what the medium itself allowed (access to a vision of a different place) (Meyrowitz 1986, p. 201).

Barbie Zelizer takes up Meyrowitz's argument in her study of media event viewing. When people view large televised events like the Olympic Games, she argues, they're using their home as a bridge to other more traditionally public domains. She writes: 'By privileging the home with the original version of the event, and by aggregating the private roles of television viewing with public roles, media events help audience blur an already existing mix of public and private' (Zelizer 1991, p. 77).

Cultural studies theorist McKenzie Wark expands this theme in *Virtual Geography* when he argues that one of the central paradoxes of the Western liberal tradition of democracy is that, while it maintains the fiction of a separation of public and private spheres, it has actually presided over the massive penetration of the public sphere, via televisual media, into the private space of the home (Wark 1994, p. 71).

This blurring of boundaries between the private sphere of the home and the public sphere of the outside world is more than actual—it has also had an important symbolic impact on the issues we regard as 'political' or worthy of community concern. When he announced his retirement in

1996, United States tabloid talk-show host Phil Donahue was interviewed by a number of high-brow journalists, some of whom asked him why he hadn't used his influence and high ratings to 'bring more politics' to the daytime masses. Donahue consistently answered that his show was all *about* politics and that he'd been ahead of the journalistic pack in featuring issues which mattered to women and other marginalised groups.

Donahue's point is that tabloid television formats like talk shows are not about the erosion of democracy—they reflect new formations of it. We're no longer living in an era dominated by Habermas's ideal public sphere in which reasonable men gather to smoke their pipes and analyse public life, but it doesn't mean politics is dead. It's just not always to be found in the places we expect it to be.

Our understanding of what constitutes the political is being rethought to include issues traditionally thought of as private. Crucially, we're all becoming increasingly aware of the connections between the public and private spheres, between making a living and living with our families and between work and leisure. Feminism itself is a vital part of this redefinition of politics, both as a cause and a symptom. Feminist debate has given shape and critical life to the shifting boundaries of our public sphere. But feminists also need to recognise that feminism has itself been fuelled and partly made possible by the social changes wrought by the media.

Seven: New media, old fears

In late 1992 and early 1993, three horrifically violent and incredibly depraved new video games were poised to hit the Australian teenage market. They were *Auschwitz*, a game in which the objective is to cram as many Jews as possible into a gas chamber; *Custer's Last Stand*, in which white soldiers rape and torture Native American women; and *Night Trap*, a game in which the player's objective is to stalk, torture, rape and murder five women.

The immediate public uproar channelled via the mass media and fuelled by the concern of senior politicians like Senator Margaret Reynolds and Attorney-General Michael Lavarch was understandable. At least it would have been if the games existed. And, unless the media attention to these fictitious products has given amateur video game producers ideas, they don't.

According to the then editor of the *Sydney Morning Herald*'s computer section, Gareth Powell, *Auschwitz* and *Custer's Last Stand* are 'definitely urban myths'. In a column published in both the *Sydney Morning Herald* and the *Age*, he wrote that he'd spent 'a considerable amount of time and money checking 400 newspapers and magazines worldwide

for real [commercially produced] versions of these games'
and had 'scoured the electronic bulletin boards of the world'.
He also offered to donate $100 to charity if any reader could
produce evidence either game existed. No-one came forward
with conclusive evidence.

Certainly, the two major retailers of video games in
Australia, Sega and Nintendo—who between them control
almost 100 per cent of the world market—do not make or
market the games. Marketing manager of Nintendo at the
time Mike Pelman told me in an interview for this book
that: 'I've never seen the games and we're very in touch with
products in the market. They are certainly not being sold
as packaged cartridge games and standard retailers wouldn't
touch them with a ten-foot pole. If they do exist at all,
they've been put out by a backyard operator on floppy disk
and retailers don't want to deal with that sort of product.'

A game manufactured by Sega entitled *Night Trap* does
exist but it bears no resemblance to the video game 'nasty'
which had radio talk-show hosts salivating. The real *Night
Trap* is based on a plot common to many widely available
B-grade horror films in which a group of aliens attack a
group of holiday-makers in their home. In one scene a
woman is captured and killed by the aliens, as are plenty of
the male characters, but the game contains no sex or sexualised violence. The player is encouraged to save the people
in the house—not stalk, torture or rape them. I can vouch
for this because I spent an entire afternoon at Sega's Sydney
offices watching a highly skilled teenage player working his
way through all the different levels of the game.

But, as is often the case in the violence-in-the-media
debate, the protagonists were careful not to let the facts spoil

their own violent fantasies. Radio 2GB announcer Russell Powell described *Night Trap* as a game in which 'the ultimate prize is to torture a woman and murder her'. The same announcer prefaced a conversation with Senator Margaret Reynolds, the chair of a senate committee set up to examine 'community standards relevant to the supply of services utilising electronic technologies', by describing the game as one in which 'five scantily clad women' were 'mutilated by all kinds of gadgets'. In response, Senator Reynolds leapt to the defence of community standards, but lost her footing on the question of technology. Asked if *Night Trap* is a video game, she replied: 'Right. Well, you see, that is precisely what our committee's about. It . . . it's trying to keep up with the technology.'

Confusion and moral panic over new technology is hardly new. What's disturbing about the recent ink and airtime lost over fictional video game 'nasties' is the failure of many feminist leaders to seize this moment of social uncertainty to articulate a feminist vision of the new technology and its role in our social and economic lives. Joining a reactive chorus of social conservatives whose only strategies for dealing with the future seem to be Ban it, Restrict and Hope It Goes Away, isn't going to win feminism many points with young women who've grown up with new media and computer technology. Like any political movement or philosophy, feminism needs to develop positive platforms on new cultural and social phenomenon. Not doing so amounts to giving other political interests and institutions the chance to make social policy unimpeded.

But there's an even more compelling reason for feminists to take a fresh and constructive look at the social and political implications of new media technology—it has important implications for feminism itself. In the previous chapter, I argued that the mass media and broadcast television in particular have been important factors in the collapse of boundaries between the private and the public spheres, and that this collapse in turn helped liberate women from a rigidly gendered social and economic order. In this chapter, I want to explore the impact new media technology is having on social relations and the way we understand ourselves.

THE BOYS' TOYS MYTH

Technology, whether we're talking cars or computers, is often regarded with suspicion in popular feminist debate. Machines are seen as a form of mechanised masculinity. They're boys' toys, designed by men to do men's work—going global, going fast and going to war. They're a tool of the patriarchy.

In *Feminism Confronts Technology* Judy Wacjman argues there is a close affinity between technology and what she terms 'the dominant ideology of masculinity' (Wacjman 1993). In her effort to establish this link, Wacjman examines the work of a range of authors, from Sherry Turkle, who once argued there are clear differences in the way males and females approach and use computers and that computer culture is 'peculiarly male in spirit, peculiarly unfriendly to women', to Bob Connell, who argues that machine-related skills and, by extension, the control of technology are fundamental to the dominant masculine archetype.

But there are a number of problems with this simple boys and techno-toys equation. The first and most important is that women, not men, have often been in the front line when it comes to dealing with new technology. As office workers, service industry employees and the people who've done the bulk of cooking and cleaning in the home, women have been expert users of some of the most important technology of the twentieth century, from microwave ovens and vacuum cleaners, to word processing software and photocopiers. To suggest women are not technology literate means ignoring the bulk of human–machine interface which goes on in daily life.

But that's precisely what's traditionally happened. Technological literacy has been defined *against* the kind of skills women have developed in the workplace and home. In the same way that traditionally female jobs have been devalued because women do them, technology women use and understand gets downgraded to the status of 'domestic appliances' or 'labour-saving devices'. Being able to navigate a word-processing program isn't interfacing with technology, it's secretarial work. Taking the top off a computer to install extra RAM, on the other hand, supposedly takes real skill.

It's a circular definitional problem which reflects another. At the heart of the privileged relationship between masculinity and technology is a self-reflexive definition of masculinity itself. Wacjman acknowledges this when she writes that 'the ideology of masculinity is remarkably flexible . . . Masculinity is expressed both in terms of muscular physical strength and aggression, and in terms of analytical power' (Wacjman 1993, pp. 146–6). The link between masculinity and technology, in other words, is reversible on demand. The idea that the mind is superior to the body is effortlessly inverted when it comes to applauding the clearly sensual pleasures of handling heavy, fast or smart machinery. In the action movie fantasy, men are always in control of the machines, never the reverse.

It's a doublethink which is even mirrored in the way we think about men and women interacting with exactly the same technology. To use an everyday example, consider the gender stereotypes which circulate around television watching. When men watch television they're popularly seen to be *doing* something. Processing important news and current affairs information. Supporting their home football team or analysing the game of their favourite tennis player. Getting involved in an action movie. The world of men's television is dominated by statistics, facts and hard information. When women watch television, everything magically changes. Female viewers are often painted as passive, easily manipulated and addicted to their favourite programs. They weep at romantic comedies. They can't do without their daily dose of soap opera. They're conned into buying useless products by home-shopping channels.

Of course, in daily life these stereotypes aren't hard and fast. Women tell their male partners off for being passive couch potatoes too. And men get their teenage daughters to reprogram the VCR. My point is that social myths can support amazing contradictions quite effortlessly and that gender and technology is an area suffused with mythology.

Confronted with the circular logic which has dominated thinking about gender and technology, it's very easy to accept the masculinity–technology equation as a given and then dismiss technology as the inevitable result of everything which is wrong with patriarchy. But it's an argument which leaves women sinking slowly back down into the passenger's seat, rolling their eyes and passing the Minties.

In her recent book on women and cyberspace, *Nattering on the Net*, prolific Australian feminist writer Dale Spender signals an important new direction in the popular feminist debate on new media and information technology. A convert to cyberspace, Spender takes a cautiously optimistic look at the way the internet and other new media is changing our lives and our sense of who we are. Unfortunately, she falls back on some gender stereotypes in support of her claim that women interact very differently with new technology to men. Discussing the prevalence of cyberporn and sexual flirtation on the net, Spender frequently makes the assumption that such pursuits only interest men. She casts women as the moral housekeepers of cyberspace:

> This is where women have a great contribution to make.
>
> It is to be regretted that some of the worst aspects of real life have become prominent features of the virtual world. But women have a history of admirable achievements when it comes to establishing a more egalitarian society. What we now face is a bigger task in our efforts to change the world: because now that we have cyberspace, we have a bigger world and more to change (Spender 1995, p. 212).

Spender's assumption that women have no interest in pornography or sexually explicit exchanges with strangers is directly contradicted by United States writer Kathy Acker's account of how she got thrown off the Net by the America On-Line service (AOL).

I was on-line with a friend. We were a little drunk, and

I can't remember what the hell we did. She had never been on-line before, so I said, 'OK, I'll show you what it's like, although AOL is so boring' . . . I think we asked if there were any dykes in the room, that's my only memory . . . Americans are so moralistic (Cross 1995a, p. 13).

Spender's claim that the 'dehumanised' sexual experiences offered by virtual porn are 'a very different thing from the personal relationships that women have indicated as their preference' (1995, p. 257), ignores the way technology has and is changing our understanding of gender, sexuality and our bodies. What women want or who they are is neither universal or essential. From the birth-control pill to the laptop computer, technology is deeply implicated in our understanding of the relationship between our minds, bodies and our gender.

While Dale Spender's attempt to develop a feminist framework for understanding the significance of the internet is admirable, her book ultimately misses the real significance of new media technology. Spender fixates on content, when what's required is a structural understanding of the impact of recent information technology—an analysis, in other words, of how new media reorganises existing avenues of communication and ultimately our social relations and notions of self.

Cultural studies scholar Sadie Plant arrives at the opposite conclusion to Spender about women and new media technology. According to Plant, there's a longstanding relationship between information technology and women's liberation—'You can almost map them onto each other in the whole history of modernity. Just as machines get more intelligent, so women get more liberated' (Cross 1995, p. 18). As Plant points out, the real problem for many women these days is not how to get access to a computer, but how to sift through the enormous daily influx of images and information.

Plant also argues that, far from reinforcing traditional masculine values, the net tends to dissolve gender boundaries. Her argument makes sense. The internet is a vast warehouse of information which isn't catalogued according to age, gender or any other traditional hierarchy. The net's only gatekeeping requirements are that the user have basic literacy and keyboard skills and access to a computer and modem. One great advantage of the net is that it allows women to access information and experiment with new interests anonymously. There are no signs saying 'Men's Magazines' and no store clerks, club members or experts standing over their shoulder making them uncomfortable. On the net, women (and men) can choose to conceal their gender and play at being the opposite sex. And there's widespread anecdotal evidence that plenty do.

In her latest book, *Life on the Screen*, Sherry Turkle moves away from her earlier arguments about gender and technology. Instead of focusing on the way men and women relate to cyberspace, she looks at the way cyberspace relates to notions of gender. How, she asks, are computers encouraging us to re-evaluate our identities in the age of the internet? What's the relationship between the virtual worlds of MUDs (multiuser domains) in which men and women routinely swap genders and even species (people play rabbits and frogs, for instance) and real life gender politics?

Drawing on two decades of observation and interviews with male and female computer users and internet habitués,

Turkle argues that gender swapping in cyberspace encourages people to confront the way gender affects the way we view others and ourselves. To pass as another gender for any length of time, she argues, 'requires understanding of how gender inflects speech, manner, the interpretation of experience' (Turkle 1996, p. 212). She describes the experience of a number of women and men who have played characters of the opposite sex and often had virtual sex while inhabiting this other gender. She concludes that these experiences often confront players with some very difficult questions about sexuality and identity. They're forced to ask of net sex, for instance:

> Is it the physical action? Is it the emotional intimacy of someone other than one's primary partner? Is infidelity in the head or in the body? Is it in the desire or in the action? . . . The fact that the physical body has been factored out of the situation makes these issues both subtler and harder to resolve than before (Turkle 1996, p. 225).

Virtual life emerges in Turkle's book as a vast experimental space, in which people are constantly pushing against the limits of their identities and those of others. Her research suggests it's very difficult to make universal claims about what women want from new media—something Dale Spender often does. Writing about violent video games, for instance, Spender asserts that young girls don't like them because 'girls are interested in personal relationships' and in 'the ongoing story of existence'. She cites an emotional experience of her own as evidence: 'Even now I can recall the terrrible effect that the demise of Judy in *Seven Little*

Australians had on me . . . I dread to think what would have happened had I been exposed to all those killer conquest computer games' (Spender 1995, p. 186).

It's not surprising Spender summons up her own childhood through a book. Novels, not television programs, MTV, action movies, video games or the internet, were the popular culture of Spender's generation. The result is a profoundly different relationship to image culture and technology—one which cannot be simply recycled to decipher contemporary media. By looking seriously at how gender nuances the production and consumption of contemporary popular cultural formats, Spender has made an important contribution to the Australian feminist debate. The next step is to begin thinking about how the production and consumption of those formats are influencing gender.

LIFE AFTER TELEVISION

In 1995, a now famous 'cyberporn' issue of *Time* magazine hit the newsstands bearing a cover image of a child with large, staring eyes illuminated by a computer screen. Children are the traditional mascots of community concern about new media, and the internet has been no exception.

In 1996, the New South Wales Attorney-General, Jeff Shaw, announced legislation that will make it an offence to transmit or retrieve material unsuitable for minors over the internet. His proposal mirrors legislation which has already been passed in the United States in response to widespread community concern about paedophilia and child pornography. Feminists in Australia and the United States have backed concerns about the potentially damaging effects of the internet on children and adolescents. Their fears about children and the internet revolve around two main issues: that paedophiles will use the internet to contact and prey on children, and that children will stumble on or seek out sexually explicit material.

Turning to concerns about paedophilia first, it's important to avoid letting the intense community concern about the sexual abuse of children dictate the way we assess the size of the actual risk. The first major United States assault on cyberporn began with an extensive FBI sting aimed at identifying and arresting paedophiles on the net. After an extensive undercover operation, federal agents swooped on more than 125 homes and offices to seize computers and disks from people suspected of trafficking in child porn over the America On-Line network. Despite two years of work and access to the private e-mail of an unknown number of America On-Line subscribers (on the basis of court orders), the FBI only arrested fifteen of those people for trafficking in paedophilic material. A number of the arrests, according to the *New York Times*, occurred as a result of active entrapment by agents. In one case, an adult investigator posing as a teenage girl convinced a Las Vegas man to cross state lines to have sex. Apart from adults responding to active solicitations by FBI agents, no-one was arrested for trying to make contact with an actual child.

United States Attorney-General Janet Reno defended the use of entrapment and declared that the government was 'not going to permit exciting new technology to be misused to exploit and injure children'.

The United States experience suggests that the group of adults who use the net to actively solicit sexual encounters with minors is negligible. But if we agree that even the tiniest risk of such an encounter is unacceptable, the question still remains how best to prevent one, short of dismantling the internet? Legislation banning sexual material on the internet isn't going to stop adults approaching kids in chat rooms, since paedophiles are unlikely to risk frightening children off with explicitly sexual banter.

It makes more sense to treat the virtual community of the internet the same way we treat the real life community. We routinely warn children about the danger of giving strangers too much information. We caution them about the hazards of talking to people they don't know on the telephone, on public transport and in the local park. We tell them not everyone can be trusted. Keeping children safe from exploitation is an ongoing process. Adults, particularly parents, have to work with children and help them negotiate unfamiliar information, situations and people. The same is true of the internet.

The second major concern about the internet is that children will stumble on or seek out sexually explicit material. The response to date has focused on banning the transmission of this material outright. But is this really a practical or socially just approach to the problem?

Responding to proposed New South Wales legislation banning sexual material on the internet, McKenzie Wark points out that if the government is going to be consistent it better start policing lots of other everyday communications, including phone calls. He writes:

> You have to choose to visit an internet site. It is not like flicking on the remote and suddenly seeing an image in your living room. This is why it is not appropriate to

treat the internet as if it were a broadcast media . . .
What the community and lawmakers need to understand
is that in terms of the amount of individual decision
needed to see something the internet is much more like
a library than like television, and should be treated
accordingly (Wark 1996, p. 11).

Wark goes on to argue that, rather than trying to make a
vast and diverse medium like the internet safe for young
children, we should think about ways of making it safer for
eight year olds to interact with an adult medium. One
obvious solution is to develop methods for classifying information and limiting children's access to adult internet sites.

In 1995, United States software producers, publishers and
on-line services formed a consortium called the Platform for
Internet Content Selection aimed at doing exactly that—creating technology standards needed to filter pornography and
other 'questionable' material from the net. The consortium
includes such corporate giants as Microsoft, Apple, Netscape,
AT&T, MCA and America On-Line. Adult internet sites
have already shown a willingness to cooperate with this
move. As US magazine, *Interactive Week*, reported, Surfwatch
(a Californian company which already makes software that
blocks sites unsuitable for children) now receives an average
of 250 calls a week from operators of adult sites asking to
be rated. Many of these sites even proudly display the ratings
mark on their home page.

But concerns about children and the internet may not
be amenable to such simple solutions, since they point to
some broader cultural anxieties about the way the labile world
of the internet and the possibilities of virtual life are changing traditional social hierarchies, including the boundaries

between adults, adolescents and children. Print media culture is grounded in the belief that there are appropriate reading materials and concepts for each age group. It's a philosophy which is reflected in both book and journal design (books for readers under 18 are labelled according to age group and magazines are similarly targeted) and access (some publications are restricted and libraries and bookshops display them in age-sensitive categories). It's a culture which has also influenced the way adults monitor children's consumption of other media, such as television and videos.

Access to power is dependent on access to information in contemporary society. Children learn this early—to move up a class in school is to move another step up the ladder of status and power. It's for this reason kids often harass adults to give them access to books, games or television programs considered 'too old' for them. But the flood of new media formats—including cable television, videos, video games, computer software and CD-ROMs—has made the job of filtering information increasingly difficult. There's more of it and lots of it is buried in forms adults are often unfamiliar with.

The internet and its progeny the World Wide Web represent the apotheosis of this trend. A vast and increasingly user-friendly international network of computers, the net directly undermines the graduated and hierarchical world of print media. There's no preordained order of information on the net—cruising it is all about making lateral connections. Every search pulls up surprising new sites and information. And while you do have to actively search out a site, access to the internet itself is just a matter of having a modem, a computer and a service provider.

Australian senator, Hedley Chapman, epitomised this concern when he told federal parliament:

> The danger for our children, *many of whom are much more computer literate than their parents* [emphasis added], is simply that by using a personal computer connected to the internet they can gain access to specific pornographic bulletin board services such as Kinknet and Throbnet often without the knowledge or permission of their parents . . .' (Australian Senate 1995, p. 1216).

The net certainly offers children and adolescents unprecedented access to different realities in a virtual form. And it's a freedom which is obviously accompanied by some risk—the question is whether the enormous community concern about the internet is solely related to risk to children or are adults also protecting themselves?

It's a question which touches on others which lie in the realm of feminist ethics. Feminism has focused attention on the role power plays in heterosexual relationships and, by extension, in any relationship where one party has formal or implicit power. Some feminists argue there can be no meaningful consent in any sexual relationship where there is a power imbalance. It's a position which has been widely criticised for actually taking power away from women and others in subordinate positions. Katie Roiphe (1993) argues, for instance, that attempts to regulate sexual interactions between college students infantilise women and treat them like helpless victims. Similarly, there is a danger that when adults act as the protectors of children's rights, particularly of children's right to their innocence, they are actually disempowering them.

In her collected essays, *Public Sex*, Pat Califia traces the roots of a late seventies campaign against child pornography and paedophilia in the United States to a backlash against the emerging gay and lesbian battle for civil rights. Many of those campaigning for children's rights, she argues, actually supported highly paternalistic models of child rearing and were mainly concerned to stop teenagers getting access to sex education or alternative models of sexuality. A paradox becomes apparent here if we consider the other side of fears about the internet: the concern about children getting access to sexual material. Pat Califia sums it up when she writes: 'Culturally induced schizophrenia allows parents to make sentimental speeches about the fleeting innocence of childhood and the happiness of years unburdened by carnal lust—and then exhaust themselves policing the sex lives of their children' (Califia 1994, p. 39). When we protect children, in other words, we need to ask whose interests we are protecting. It's one thing to shield a young child from the sexual attentions of a paedophile, but it's arguably quite another to 'protect' a 15-year-old boy from his own homosexual desires.

The anxiety about children being exposed to adult sexuality is unavoidably bound up with broader anxieties about the potential new media has to change people and traditional social power structures and values. The fear that children are being corrupted (made adult before their time) goes hand in hand with the fear that modern adults are too childish (they spend too much time eating junk food, watching videos and generally attending to short-term wants). Popular feminist debate on new media is too often dominated by a reactive maternalism which constructs feminists as the harried protectors of women and children. It's a position, as I argue in chapter one, which puts them in the company of right-wing politicians and religious fundamentalists. If television and the rise of mediated communication helped blur the boundaries between the public and the private spheres, the internet is blurring the ones between real life and virtual existence. When we boot up our laptops and connect with the World Wide Web we create a virtual extension of ourselves which reaches out beyond the physical space we inhabit. We're splitting ourselves from our bodies and sending this disembodied self off to play in a world where gender, race and sexuality cannot be read off the surface of our texts.

Like all new media, the interface between the virtual and the real world mapped out in the internet is drawing apocalyptic and utopian claims. But what's required, in the long run, is a willingness to ask questions.

Eight: Feminist politics in the media future

In the updated edition of her feminist classic *Damned Whores and God's Police*, Anne Summers includes an 'open letter to the next generation' in which she asks younger women why they're so alienated by feminists of her era. She recalls how horrified she was to discover many younger women haven't made the connection 'between the great array of choices now available' to women 'and the battles we had fought'. And she asks of a hypothetical young woman who 'wanted to do something with her life':

> Wouldn't she acknowledge this? Wouldn't she feel some-thing—gratitude? a debt? a responsibility to keep widening those choices for herself and her generation? To me, it seemed inconceivable that young women in their early twenties would not be as drawn to the movement to increase women's opportunities as I had been when I was their age (Summers 1994, p. 506)

A former editor-in-chief of *Ms* magazine and a legendary Australian feminist bureaucrat, Summers has a broad knowl-edge of the history and politics of both Australian and United States feminism. As a sought-after public figure and senior magazine editor, she also has daily contact with intelligent and independent young women. Yet she seems genuinely perplexed—almost shocked—by many of their priorities and attitudes.

Summers goes on to suggest reasons for this reality gap—reasons I address below. But the real answer to her question is already buried in her own open letter. It's there in the confidence with which she speaks of 'the women's movement', as if it were still a unified cause with universal goals. It's there in her casual references to 'activism' as if the political strategies which worked in the 1970s are still appropriate and effective. And most of all it's there in Summers' failure to see what it is the next generation(s) of feminists *are* doing with their lives.

It would be unfair to attack Summers herself for some purported failure to understand another generation's concerns. In publishing her open letter, she's simply going public with perceptions held by many other second wave feminists. And she voices her concerns with a tone of genuine inquiry. But it's a tone which also highlights a curious absence in her text—a failure to acknowledge the implications her own generational power has had for younger feminists coming up through the ranks.

Like other prominent feminists of her era, Summers now speaks from a position of immense authority. She's a powerbroker in an unofficial but highly influential political network spawned by the women's movement of the 1970s. A network which includes judges, politicians, senior media figures, lawyers, key bureaucrats and public intellectuals. A lobby group with the power to get federal legislation passed and undesirable elements of the media censored. A group of high-profile public figures who are more or less guaranteed the moral high ground in mainstream media coverage.

Of course, few younger feminists would have it otherwise. As Summers correctly points out, without this influential public-sphere feminist network, many of the basic gains of the women's movement would never have occurred. The problem is that many feminists of Summers' generation are slow to acknowledge the consequences of the power they've acquired. They're unable, or unwilling, to see feminism itself as a system, with institutionalised rhetorics, priorities, and techniques for disciplining the ranks. Younger feminists, however well versed they might be in the intellectual and activist history of the seventies, can find themselves in a very tenuous position if they try to buck this system. Indeed, from where the next generation(s) of feminists stand, the old guard can look an awful lot like the patriarchy.

Like patriarchs, some senior feminists are inclined to think they represent, and speak for, women as a whole. And, like patriarchs, they legitimise their claim to power by arguing they are only holding on to it for the benefit of 'womankind'. They sometimes dismiss arguments which undermine the ideological positions bolstering their own institutional power as insufficiently schooled in the bigger feminist picture—as deficient in the lessons of history.

It's tempting to attribute this stand-off to a generation gap—a simple case of daughters challenging their mothers. In reality, though, contemporary feminism has fractured along a series of fault lines which have little to do with age and experience and far more to do with a debate, which germinated in the eighties and has intensified in the nineties, over the shape and future of feminist ethics. It's a debate I discuss at length later in this chapter, but it's worth noting here that one of its chief concerns—the way feminist power has become institutionalised—goes to the heart of why many younger feminists may *perceive* a generation gap.

In just over a quarter of a century, feminism has become an institution. There are now thousands of books detailing the theoretical and practical turns the movement took in the seventies. Basic issues affecting women, such as domestic violence, child care, health issues, sex discrimination, sexual harassment and equal pay have evolved into key public-sphere issues dealt with in legislation, common law, government reports and academic inquiries. Many universities have departments devoted to women's studies and a host of other tertiary courses now incorporate feminist theory. There are still plenty of important battles to be fought on behalf of women, but the logistics of fighting them have been largely taken out of the hands of ordinary women and consigned to the domain of government departments and experts in the legal, medical and academic spheres.

Domestic violence is a good example—in her open letter Summers recalls her personal involvement in establishing the first women's refuge in Australia. Today, there is a publicly funded refuge infrastructure, widespread media awareness of the problem of domestic violence and hundreds of reports and recommendations on the subject. To become usefully involved in the area today it's not enough to be a feminist—you need qualifications and a career path.

The point isn't that younger feminists needn't care about domestic violence or ought to consider the problem 'solved', but rather that the sense of community which flows from hands-on involvement in identifying and fixing a social problem is simply not part of their common experience. Feminism has become a specialised field as much as a movement—the demands of older generation feminists have become policy goals embedded in our public and private institutions. Participating in implementing these goals requires an increasing level of expertise.

The answer to the question of why some younger feminists fail to identify with the women's movement as a whole may be bound up with the success older feminists have had in getting central feminist concerns taken seriously. Younger feminists have had to focus their concerns in specialised areas and integrate feminist theory into wider institutions and disciplines. This need to integrate our identity as feminists with specialist fields has also led to a shift in the form and meaning of 'activism'. Feminists can no longer credibly claim to be 'outside' the system. Summers describes this shift in reference to her own career:

> Like most of my contemporaries in the movement, I viewed the media with suspicion, especially as it seemed so hostile to our cause, and we regarded government mainly as a source of funds in return for which we felt we were expected to prune our radicalism to fit existing policies. I would never have guessed back then that I would spend the next sixteen years moving between government and the media (Summers 1994, p. 3).

The institutionalisation of feminism has profoundly complicated feminist identity. Feminists find themselves both inside and outside their discipline or profession—they are feminists *and* philosophers; news journalists *and* feminists.

The conjunction is not as simple as it looks. A feminist lawyer who sets out to challenge the gender bias in the application of a provocation defence to murder, for instance, will find herself challenging more than a simple defence. Eventually, she will find herself challenging foundational concepts in the Western legal system like 'the reasonable man' (and its implicit corollary, 'the irrational woman'). But to mount this kind of challenge with any effectiveness or credibility she will have to spend years gaining an understanding of the existing system and working her way into its elite ranks. Paradoxically, for many feminists, changing systems often means becoming a valued part of them.

The mainstreaming of feminist issues has not only profoundly changed the professional opportunities open to many women, but their personal relationships as well. Summers recalls her experience at *Ms* magazine, when a number of younger writers expressed their fear of winding up childless like their mentors—a choice she notes many older feminists made consciously and proudly.

> I had looked around at my colleagues at *Ms.* and seen a group of strong, independent women, with great jobs, in control of their lives and who I assumed considered themselves far better off than any previous generation of women . . . *They* [the younger women] had looked at us and seen a bunch of sad and lonely people who lived only for their jobs and their politics . . . (Summers 1994, p. 507)

This kind of direct generational comparison ignores the seismic structural shifts which have taken place in society in the interim. The women's movement has helped change the very meaning of marriage, maternity and sexuality. While we are still far from a society in which all men take equal share of domestic and family responsibilities, there is now a broad cross-section of younger men who have grown up with and accept basic feminist values. Heterosexual relationships are no longer polarised by the pain of recent social change and some younger feminists are able to view them with renewed optimism. The growing economic independence of Australian women, along with access to contraception, abortions and a more just family law system, means that more women are able to walk away from relationships that aren't working to their advantage—and there is every evidence that they are doing just that. Divorce rates have boomed since the early seventies and many women choose to simply live with partners rather than marry them. More women are also having children later in life and returning to full-time work soon after giving birth. Of course, women are still far from equal with men in the workplace and are often expected to do more than their equal share of work in the home. But it is simplistic to suggest that young feminists see a straightforward choice between embracing feminism and a career or having a long-term relationship and a family.

If younger women really are too quick to 'mouth that anthem of the 80s, "I'm not a feminist but . . ."' (Summers 1994, p. 510), it may have a lot more to do with a distaste for a reactive victim rhetoric and an intolerance for the generalisations about men and heterosexuality which dog feminist debate. Younger feminists are arguably conscious of rather than complacent about their inheritance—their refusal to identify as victims is bound up with their acceptance of the new independence and opportunities now available to them.

THEORY AND PRACTICE: WHAT'S LEFT?

Recalling a speech made by Women's Liberation Movement veteran Juliet Mitchell in the mid-'70s, Meaghan Morris describes a moment which will be gratingly familiar to anyone who's tried to talk 'theory' to a group of feminists who believe that what they do is 'practice'. 'Mitchell', Morris writes, 'completed a generous and enlightening lecture on her work, only to be greeted instantly with that voice, that nightmare voice of the Left, yelling boldly from up the back of the room, "Yeh, Juliet what about Chile?"' (Morris 1988, p. 180).

Morris told this anecdote as part of a paper she gave in 1986 analysing the stand-off between the traditional left and contemporary cultural theory, which includes a bundle of ideas often labelled as 'poststructuralist'. The paper reads as if Morris is speaking to people on a neighbouring icefloe which has only recently come adrift from the bit she's standing on. A faint, if characteristically strategic, 'we' hovers over her talk. Her tone is by turns affectionate, acerbic, irritable and solicitous. She's talking to people with whom she shares some history. People who ought to trust her ends if they don't understand her means. She's talking to family.

Ten years later, the fracture Morris diagnosed is a gulf. Not only is there scant communication between feminists who do theoretical work on cultural and political questions and those involved in the public policy sphere, there is frequently open hostility.

In the course of diagnosing the origins of this now chronic rift in the left, Morris sketches out a very useful microhistory of the relationship between leftist intellectuals and activism in Australia. Unlike Summers, who grows nostalgic about 'lifestyle' leftism, Morris analyses the material conditions which gave rise to an apparent organic connnection between theory and practice. She argues that in 1975 'cultural politics were the concern of the *full-time radical*' and that it was 'a matter of taking politics *to* various cultural activities', but that by 1985, 'the full-time radical has in many cases become the radical professional—operating in a fairly narrow but precisely defined sphere of activity, with "politics" increasingly defined by, and in terms of, the day-to-day conflict structuring that (usually institutional) activity' (Morris 1988, p. 176).

A writer whose work has appeared in everything from daily newspapers to elite academic journals, Morris has a keen sense of the diffuse networks which link academic theory, popular debate and everyday life. One consequence is her concern with developing speaking strategies which challenge social and cultural conventions about what it's *possible* to say.

The separation between theory and practice, Morris rightly suggests, is artificial. Theory must be understood as its own form of practice. Ideas act on the world, particularly in a world in the grip of an information revolution. They make meaning of cultural institutions and practices. And, while ideas produce things, practice is conversely always underpinned by ideas and constrained by the quality of those ideas. The idea that theory and practice are separate has more to do with people's perceptions of what it is they do, than the impact of their work on 'the real world'. Unfortunately, perceptions can sometimes amount to reality when it comes to lines of communication.

In her book on Australian feminism, *Gender Shock*, United States feminist Hester Eisenstein observes that 'by far the most significant difference between Australian and American feminism' is 'the degree to which Australian feminists . . . found their way into public positions of influence' (Eisenstein 1991, p. 11). Analysing the reasons for the bureaucratisation of Australian feminism, Eisenstein suggests it was partly a result of career obstacles in the academic world 'which had not—in strong contrast to the United States—created a world of Women's Studies to welcome, or at least make some grudging room for, self-proclaimed feminist academics' (1991, p. 13).

Eisenstein's claim that universities drove feminism away says more about a rift between sections of the feminist academy and bureaucracy, than it does about the status of Women's Studies in Australian universities. The introduction of Women's Studies and other feminists units into Australian universities certainly engendered fierce battles—the most public of which concerned the right of Elizabeth Jacka and Jean Curthoys to teach a course on philosophy and feminism in the Sydney University philosophy department. The university-wide strike which ensued ended in a victory for staff and students who wanted the course, but saw the philosophy department split literally in two. But Women's Studies units were offered in three Australian universities in the early seventies. And the abolition of student fees by the Whitlam government brought an influx of female students, particularly mature-age women, into tertiary institutions. By the time Eisenstein arrived in 1980, the fruits of the turbulent marriage between feminism and the Australian academy were already apparent in the work of an ideologically diverse group of writers and scholars such as—Judith Allen, Ann Curthoys, Rosalyn Diprose, Moira Gatens, Helen Grace, Elizabeth Grosz, Jill Julius Matthews, Meaghan Morris, Carole Pateman and Rosemary Pringle. The virtual invisibility of the debates between these thinkers in Eisenstein's book, which purports to document Australian feminism, illustrates how much a Chinese wall had already developed between the Australian 'femocracy' and certain sections of the feminist academy.

It's a complicated rift—and one which (unfortunately for the sake of this narrative) doesn't divide neatly along institutional lines. Its essence is suggested by a comment Eisenstein made in 1987, when she told a sociology conference that: 'Some [feminists] are immersing themselves in a poststructuralist world view where the achievements of feminism have no meaning because the terrain of political stuggle has been abandoned for the terrain of discourse' (Eisenstein 1991, p. 33). The feminists Eisenstein is criticising here are mainly, but not exclusively, academy-based. And while they are by no means a homogenous group, they are loosely bound together by a mutual interest in rethinking cultural and political theory in a way which questions universalising ideas about truth and power. They are often described as 'poststructuralist' or 'postmodernist' because their work participates in a global, interdisciplinary critique of modernist or post-Enlightenment ideas about reason, history, culture and politics. [I would need a separate book to give even a brief overview of the significance and diversity of feminist work in this area—but I can offer this book as one example of work that has been influenced by postmodern/poststruturalist theory.]

Despite at least a decade of publishing and public debate, poststructuralist feminists are still frequently dismissed as apolitical or simply idiotic by feminists in the legislative, judicial and policy-making arena—a complex and diverse debate about the nature of feminist identity, ethics and politics get reduced to banal parody. Poststructuralist feminists are commonly said to indulge in 'Francobabble' or to think 'everything's relative'. In fact, feminists immersed in the 'poststructuralist world' Eisenstein is so quick to dismiss in the above quote, have a lot to offer feminists working with, and on behalf of, the state. Much poststructuralist feminist work is directly concerned with interactions between the contemporary state, power and knowledge—issues which, as Eisenstein herself notes, present important questions for women working in public policy and government. Contrary to her claim they've 'abandoned' political struggles, many poststructuralist feminists have expended a great deal of energy reconsidering what battles are important and how and where they should be waged. They reject the idea that power only resides in monolithic centralised institutions like our courts and parliaments and are more interested in the way it permeates everyday life. To give one example, Australian feminist philosophers Moira Gatens and Elizabeth Grosz have both built international reputations with their work on sexual difference and the body, and their research has delivered clear policy-making implications for issues like women's health, medical ethics and reproductive rights under the law.

One of the key concerns of poststructuralist feminism is the difficulty of simply 'using' existing systems to further feminist goals. The feminist attempt to find a legal solution to pornography illustrates some of the perils of trying to bend existing power structures to feminist goals. In 1982, United States antipornography campaigner Catharine MacKinnon emphatically rejected the role of the patriarchal state and the common law in furthering the interests of women (MacKinnon 1982, p. 3). But she has since enthusiastically touted legislative solutions to pornography and even courted conservative legislators for this purpose. MacKinnon has apparently come to believe the ends justify the means. But as I mentioned in chapter five the MacKinnon–Dworkin alliance with conservative legislators shows state power is not as easy to control as antiporn activists might think. Dworkin, along with a range of other feminist and lesbian writers, has had her work censored and banned in Canada, where a version of the MacKinnon–Dworkin censorship proposals have become law. And in the United States, the feminist-fuelled public debate over the need to censor sexually explicit material has provided a cosy niche for conservatives who want to censor women's health and family planning literature.

In Australia, public policy feminists have taken the lead in debates on contentious legislation such as the tightening of provisions in sexual harassment laws and sexual vilification. Those who mount objections are commonly sidelined as ignorant of, or hostile to, feminist concerns. Yet, the codification of feminist concerns in this kind of legislation deserves broad debate in the feminist community.

More generally, contemporary feminist theory has a great

deal to offer the Australian public debate on feminism which remains dominated by a handful of senior feminists, some of who are still wedded to feminist principles developed in the feminist debates of the 1970s.

There is truth to the claim that some feminist academics speak an obtuse language. But what is less often acknowledged is that all branches of contemporary feminism have developed a specialist rhetoric. A public policy document dealing with feminist issues in superannuation legislation can be just as difficult to follow as a philosophical argument about feminism and Spinoza. Specialist rhetoric is a necessary evil. The point is not to jettison it so we can all go back to some 'common' feminist language, but to find strategic ways of translating between the diverse institutions and disciplines which make up contemporary feminism.

CONTEMPORARY FEMINIST THEORY: A DIFFERENT KIND OF DIFFERENCE

So let's get specific. What insights can contemporary feminist theory offer to mainstream feminist politics and debate?

Feminist theory is always uneasily bound to two goals. On one hand, it has to contend with the historical male dominance of politics, philosophy, literary studies and all other knowledges. On the other, feminist scholars and writers are expected to promote the feminist struggle. The point is not that theory and practice are in opposition, but that, for feminists, intellectual rigour and political activism complicate each other. Feminism arguably challenges the claim there can be a 'disinterested' perspective on human experience—that you can't, for instance, teach feminist media studies without becoming keenly aware that the 'objectivity' which has been held up as an ideal by the quality press participates in a notion of truth made for and by men. Teaching feminist media studies is not about 'adding' a feminist perspective to the media, it's about questioning the foundation of the media from within.

One of the key conflicts in contemporary feminist theory occurs right here: in the debate between feminists who ultimately want to reposition women as the equals of men and feminists who want to theorise and build on women's difference from men and patriarchal culture. The former camp arguably includes liberal and socialist feminists who have focused on bringing down social and economic barriers to women's participation in public life. The latter stresses women's difference from men and is keen to understand this difference as autonomous and productive.

This notion of difference is not as simple as it first looks. Difference has traditionally been understood as something oppositional—male versus female, for instance, or man versus boy. This kind of difference is based on an inequality because the second term only exists to refine the first. For example, in the pair man versus woman, man functions as the neutral, self-sufficient term—the term which can stand in as a universal term—while woman is the negation of man (effectively 'not-man'). Over the past decade, feminists have tried to come up with a different understanding of difference—they've tried to think about how difference can be conceived without reference to a norm. How, in other words, can women be valued for their specificity in a way which doesn't derive its meaning from an opposition to men or patriarchy?

A politics built on this second kind of difference is interested in more than simple social structures; it implies an overhaul in the way we understand knowledge, meaning and representation. For our purposes here, it's sufficient to look at the way this strain of feminist thought has critiqued some popular assumptions derived from liberal and socialist feminism.

Over the past twenty-five years, feminists have made an enormous effort to bring women together under the banner of the women's movement and to find a common language for women to discuss their oppression. The problem, from a difference feminist perspective, is that this desire to group women under a 'we' of feminism, is entirely compatible with the universalising impulse behind patriarchal constructions of identity. It leaves no space for the way women's experiences might differ along racial, class and cultural lines. And like traditional philosophy it relies on the strategies of saming (women are the same) and othering (women are different from men) to construct identity.

From a pragmatic, political point of view, identity politics are a necessary lobbying tool. But identity has a habit of exceeding its strategic boundaries. As soon as someone invokes the general category of women, an internal debate invariably begins among feminists over what we mean by 'women'. Some extremely difficult questions follow, including: what is the relationship between sex (biology) and gender (the social meaning assigned to biology)? If gender is a social construct, are women reduced to their biology? Is the body a natural, given object or is it also cultural?

Judith Butler observes that this continual attempt to define what women have in common actually winds up promoting bitter factionalisation in the women's movement. Butler totally rejects the idea that the feminist movement should aim for a unity and instead argues that women should value disputes over questions of identity because 'this constant rifting ought to be affirmed as the ungrounded ground of feminist theory' (Butler 1992, p. 16).

Butler is setting herself up here in a position which is popularly understood as postmodern. In simple terms, she's arguing that the real strength of feminist theory lies in its potential to challenge the search for a universal truth. By refusing to centre and cement the category 'woman', feminist philosophy can act as an irritant to traditional philosophy and its assumptions about women, as well as emancipating feminism from the demand that it adhere to traditional ontological and metaphysical categories.

But if we do away with these categories, how do we ground feminism? In a concrete sense, the problem is analogous to whipping an unwanted tablecloth out from under a set of glasses—how do we remove the cloth without breaking the crystal? The problem is that in thinking about the patriarchy, feminists are forced to use a patriarchal intellectual tradition. Yet if we reject this tradition out of hand, what criteria are we going to use to judge ourselves? Or to turn the problem over, if we can't generalise about women, what's the point of feminism?

One alternative is to stop searching for a politically or theoretically pure position for feminism, and instead embrace contradictions and compromises as a strength. The future of feminism, in other words, doesn't lie in finding universally true answers, but in learning to ask the right questions at the right time. Elizabeth Grosz identifies this problem precisely when she writes:

> It is no longer a matter of maintaining a theoretical purity at the cost of political principles, nor is it simply a matter of the ad hoc adoption of theoretical principles according to momentary needs or whims. It is a question of negotiating a path between always impure positions—seeing that politics is always already bound up with what it contests (including theories)—and that theories are always implicated in various political struggles (whether this is acknowledged or not) . . . (Grosz 1995, p. 56).

One of the key insights of difference feminism may be that there is no mythical 'uncompromised' position for feminist theory and practice. Feminism is both necessitated by, and contained within, patriarchal systems. But that doesn't mean feminists have to oscillate between a reactive position and complicity with patriarchy. On the contrary, as a range of contemporary feminist theorists suggest, feminists can take traditional forms of knowledge and power and reinvent them.

FEMINISM REACHES CRITICAL MASS

In the late 1960s, two generations confronted each other across a vast cultural gap. One grew up before television, the other grew up with it. Content aside, television arguably effected one basic change in society: it gave everyone an opportunity to see worlds which they formerly had no clear picture of. The disadvantaged saw inside the homes of white middle-class families portrayed in sitcoms; women watched the public sphere—politics, corporate life, the professional privileges of men—unfold nightly on the news. Television gave everyone a backstage view of other people's lives. The Vietnam war protest movement was fuelled by it—for the first time Australian and American youth at home got to see images of a war as it happened and to contemplate the contradictions in what politicians said about it and what they were doing. Television juxtaposed political and religious rhetoric with graphic images of racism, war and brutality. And, in this sense, it helped bond a young generation, fuel a group consciousness and provide an accessible platform for getting the political message out.

Television, as I've argued throughout this book, also helped break down the domestic isolation of women in the fifties and sixties by offering them this direct window onto the public world of men. Content, or what women were told their place was by television programmers, was less important than what the medium itself allowed, access to a vision of a different place. Television is a technology which blurs the boundaries between the public and private spheres. The invisible signals which bring information and images from outside directly into our private homes have rearranged the physical walls which make up the architecture of our cities and our everyday lives.

But it's a process which was already underway with the proliferation of mass education, the improvement in print-ing production and distribution technology and the urbanisation of populations which occurred with the Indus-trial Revolution. All these factors led to the growth of an information industry which, while ostensibly promoting the ideology of patriarchy, also initiated a flow of information which initiated the erosion of the boundaries between the public and the private spheres.

This is the significance of mass-media culture for women—the need to find a mass audience for advertisers meant designing programs which spoke across the traditional boundaries of class, race and gender. While this 'lowest common denominator' homogeneity is often decried for rotting our culture, the truth is high culture always served the needs of an elite and was never fully inclusive of women. It's no accident, then, that the accelerated spread of mass culture in the sixties coincided with the eruption of politics outside the traditional public sphere—in the civil rights movements of the late sixties, the women's movement and the environmental movement. Ironically, the mass media formats which feminists have traditionally opposed and defined their values against have been a critical vehicle for feminism to communicate across gender, class and demographic boundaries, both to address other women, and to engage in critical discussion with male-defined culture and institutions.

In *Popular Reality*, John Hartley argues that the traditional public sphere is being replaced by a feminised, suburbanised, consumerist and global domain of popular media entertainment. And it's here, he suggests, in the interaction between viewers and media culture, that contemporary politics lives. Hartley sketches the birth of a new kind of public sphere—a sphere grounded in the intersection between popular culture and everyday life. A domain in which the private and the public meet (Hartley 1996).

Feminism was made possible by the silent seepage of images of public life into the private, a process which began with the growth of literacy and mass culture. Feminist politics have always been intimately concerned with connecting up these worlds. Second wave feminism, in this sense, offers something more profound than a critique of masculine public life from the point of view of values which were once confined to the private ('the personal is political'). Feminism is about re-articulating the relationship between the public and private spheres. And, consequently, feminism and the mass media occupy different sides of the same coin. Both call a symbolic public into being from the private sphere. Both tend to destabilise the relationship between these spheres. And both are the focus of broad social anxiety for precisely these reasons.

By perpetuating a view of mass media forms—from advertising to pornography—as inherently hostile to women, feminists are clinging to a literal-minded and narrow view of the relationship between the media and their consumers. Instead, we need to consider what the mass media and feminism might have in common and what feminism can learn from the mass media.

If feminism is to remain engaged with and relevant to the everyday lives of women, then feminists desperately need tools to understand everyday culture. We need to engage with debates in popular culture, rather than taking an elitist and dismissive attitude towards the prime means of communication in our society. And we need active attempts to produce diverse forms of speech, rather than reactionary campaigns to suppress speech.

References

Atkinson, M. 1994, 'Shooting Stars', *Cleo*, no. 263, September, Sydney.

Australian Senate 1995, *Debates*, no. 3, Wed. 1 March.

Australian Institute of Criminology 1990, *Violence: Directions For Australia*, Canberra.

Barnett, D. 1995, 'The Porn Industry's Quest For The Really Swinging Voter', *Good Weekend*, October 28, pp. 50–4.

Baudrillard, J. 1990, *Seduction*, St Martin's Press, New York.

Berger, J. 1986, *Ways of Seeing*, Penguin, London.

Bernstein, C. 1992, 'The Idiot Culture', *New Republic*, June 8.

Brown, W. 1995, *States of Injury: Power and Freedom in Late Modernity*, Princeton University Press, Princeton.

Burton, L. 1992, 'Don't Just Blame The Rambos', *Australian*, November 9, p. 20.

Busch, C. 1995, 'Every Man a Queen', *New York*, July 17, p. 26.

Butler, J. 1991, 'Imitation and Gender Insubordination', *Inside/Out. Lesbian Theories. Gay Theories*, ed. D. Fuss, Routledge, New York.

—— 1992, 'Contingent Foundations: Feminism and the Question of "Postmodernism"', *Feminists Theorise the Political*, eds J. Butler & R.J. Scott, Routledge, New York.

Califia, P. 1994, *Public Sex: The Culture of Radical Sex*, Cleis Press, Pittsburg.

Clark, K. 1990, *The Nude: a Study in Ideal Form*, Princeton University, Princeton.

Coleman, P. 1974, *Obscenity, Blasphemy and Sedition: 100 Years of Censorship in Australia*, Angus & Robertson, Sydney.

Coombs, A. 1996 *Sex and Anarchy: The Life and Death of the Sydney Push*, Penguin Books, Melbourne.

Cross, R. 1995a, 'Acker-On-Line', *21C*, issue 3.95, pp. 12–15.

Cross, R. 1995b, 'Cybergettes', *21C*, issue 3.95, pp. 17–19.

Crowley, R. 1993, *ABA [Australian Broadcasting Authority] Update*, no. 11, September, p. 9.

Deitz, M. 1994, 'The Shackled sex', *Australian Women's Forum*, vol. 4, no. 36.

Denfeld, R. 1995, *The New Victorians*, Warner Books, New York.

Dutton, G. & Harris, M. 1970, *Australia's Censorship Crisis*, Sun Books, Melbourne.

Dworkin, A. 1987, *Intercourse*, Free Press, New York.

—— 1992, 'Against the Male Flood: Censorship, Pornography and Equality', *Pornography: Women, Violence and Civil Liberties*, ed. C. Itzin, Oxford University Press.

Edgar, P. & McPhee, H. 1974, *Media She*, Heinemann, Melbourne.

Eisenstein, H. 1991, *Gender Shock*, Beacon Press, Boston.

Evans, R. 1977, *The Feminists*, Croom Helm, London.

Faludi, S. 1991, *Backlash: the Undeclared War Against Women*, Chatto & Windus, London.

Faust, B. 1994, *Backlash? Balderdash: Where Feminism Is Going Right*, University of New South Wales Press, Sydney.

Fillion, K. 1996, *Lip Service: the Truth about Women's Darker Side in Love, Sex and Friendship*, HarperCollins, New York.

Fiske, J. 1994, *Media Matters: Everyday Culture and Political Change*, University of Minnesota Press, Minneapolis.

Foucault, M. 1979, *The History of Sexuality*, vol. 1, Penguin, London.

France, K. 1995 'What's Wrong With Drag', *New York*, July 17, p. 30.

Frank, A. 1990, 'Bringing Bodies Back In: a Decade Review', *Theory, Culture and Society*, vol. 7, no. 1, pp. 131–62.

Garber, M. 1993, *Vested Interests: Cross-Dress and Cultural Anxiety*, Harper Perennial, New York.

Garner, H. 1995, *The First Stone: Some Questions About Sex and Power*, Picador, Sydney.

Gatens, M. 1993, *Feminism and Philosophy: Perspectives on Difference and Equality*, Polity Press, Cambridge.

—— 1996, *Imaginary Bodies: Ethics, Power and Corporeality*, Routledge, London.

Gelbart, L. 1995 'Peering Through the Tube Darkly', *New York Times*, April 16, p. 33.

Gilligan, C. 1982, *In a Different Voice: Psychological Theory and Women's Development*, Harvard University Press, Cambridge, Mass.

Grace H. & Stephen, A. 1981, 'Where Do Positive Images Come From? (And What Does a Woman Want?)', *Scarlet Woman*, no. 12, March, pp. 15–22.

Grosz, E. 1981, 'On Speaking About Pornography', *Scarlet Woman*, no. 13, Spring, pp. 16–21.

Grosz, E. 1994a, 'Sexual Difference and the Problem of Essentialism', *The Essential Difference*, eds. N. Schor, and E. Weed, Indiana University Press, Bloomington.

—— 1994b, *Volatile Bodies: Toward a Corporeal Feminism*, Allen & Unwin, Sydney.

—— 1995, *Space, Time and Perversion*, Routledge, New York.

Habermas, J. 1989, *The Structural Transformation of the Public Sphere: An Inquiry into a Category of Bourgeois Society*, trans. T. Burger, and F. Lawrence, MIT Press, Cambridge, Mass.

Hall, J. & Hall, S. 1970, *Australian Censorship: the XYZ of Love*, Jack De Lissa, Sydney.

Hallin, D. 1994, *We Keep America on Top of the World: Television Journalism and the Public Sphere*, Routledge, London.

Hartley, J. 1992, *The Politics of Pictures: the Creation of the Public in the Age of Popular Media*, Routledge, London and New York.

—— 1996, *Popular Reality: Journalism, Modernity, Popular Culture*, Edward Arnold, London.

Heaton, J. A. & Wilson, N. L. 1995, 'Tuning Into Trouble', *Ms*, September–October, pp. 45–51.

Heyn, D. 1995, 'The Affair: What To Do When You Get Caught', *Cosmopolitan*, New York, p. 155.

Hirschorn, M. 1995, 'The Myth of Pop Culture Depravity', *New York*, September 4, pp. 29–35.

Horin, A. 1984, 'Women and Pornography: the New Censors', *National Times*, March 30, pp. 12–13.

Hunter, I., Saunders, D. & Williamson, D. 1993, *On Pornography: Literature, Sexuality and Obscenity Law*, St Martin's Press, New York.

Huntley, R. 1995, 'Censuring *Salo*: the controversy over the banning of Pier Pasolini's *Salo* in Australia', an unpublished thesis, Department of Theatre Studies and Film, University of NSW, November 1995.

Irigaray, I. 1985, *This Sex Which Is Not One*, trans. Porter, C. with Burke, C., Cornell University Press, Ithaca.

Jay, M. 1994, *Downcast Eyes: The Denigration of Vision in Twentieth Century French Thought*, University of California Press, Berkeley.

Jeffreys, S. 1993, *The Lesbian Heresy*, Spinifex Press, Melbourne.

Joyrich, L. 1990, 'Critical and Textual Hypermasculinity', *Logics of Television*, ed. P. Mellencamp, Indiana University Press, Bloomington.

Kaminer, W. 1992, 'Exposing the New Authoritarians', *San Francisco Examiner*, November 29.

Kolbert, E. 1995, 'Wages of Deceit: Untrue Confessions', *New York Times*, June 11, section 2, p. 2.

Lake, M. 1993 'The Politics of Respectability: Identifying the Masculinist Context', *Debutante Nation: Feminism Contests the 1890s*, eds S. Margarey, S. Rowley, & S. Sheridan, Allen & Unwin, Sydney.

Loane, S. 1993, 'Mum, Wife, Victim: How the Media Portray Women', *Sydney Morning Herald*, July 2, p. 8.

Lumby, C. 1993, 'Media Critics Leap in the Dark', *Australian*, May 26.

—— 1994a, Interview with Gerald Stone.

—— 1994b, 'Too Violent? Television, Movies and Video Nasties', *Good Weekend*, May 21, p. 37.

—— 1994c, Interview with Duncan Chappell.

—— 1994d, Interview with John Dickie.

—— 1994e, Interview with Lisa Salmon.

McDonald, P. 1995, *Families in Australia*, Australian Institute of Family Studies, Melbourne.

MacKinnon, C. 1979, *Sexual Harassment of Working Women: a Case of Sex Discrimination*, Yale University Press, New Haven.

—— 1982, 'Feminism, Marxism, Method and the State: an Agenda for Theory', *Signs*, vol. 7, no. 3, Spring.

—— 1987, *Feminism Unmodified: Discourses on Life and Law*, Harvard University Press, Cambridge.

—— 1992, 'Pornography, Civil Rights and Speech', *Pornography, Women, Violence and Civil Liberties: a Radical New View*, ed. C. Itzin, Oxford University Press, Oxford.

Margarey, S., Rowley, S. & Sheridan, S. (eds) 1993, *Debutante Nation: Feminism Contests the 1890s*, Allen & Unwin, Sydney.

Mayer, H. 1968, *The Press in Australia*, Landsdowne Press, London.

Meyrowitz, J. 1986, *No Sense of Place*, Oxford University Press, New York.

Mifflin, L. 1995, 'Talk-Show Critics Urge Boycott of Programs by Advertisers', *New York Times*, December 8, section A, p. 22.

Morris, M. 1988, *The Pirate's Fiancée: Feminism, Reading, Postmodernism*, Verso, London.

—— 1995, Debate on censorship at Academy Twin Cinema, Sydney, February.

Mulvey, L. 1989, 'Visual Pleasure and Narrative Cinema', *Visual and Other Pleasures*, Indiana University Press, Bloomington.

Nead, L. 1992, *The Female Nude: Art, Obscenity and Sexuality*, Routledge, London.

Neville, R. 'The Kill Culture', *The Independent Monthly*, April 1993, pp. 25–7.

Nixon, R. 1989, 'Memo to President Bush: How To Use TV—And Keep From Being Abused By It', *TV Guide*, January 14.

Office of the Status of Women, 1993a, National Working Party on the Portrayal of Women in the Media position paper, AGPS, Canberra.

—— 1993b, *Women and Media*, Report of the National Working Party on the Portrayal of Women in the Media, Australian Government Printing Service, Sydney.

O'Neill, J. 1995, 'Sex and Violence and the New Censors', *Independent Monthly*, May, pp. 60–6.

Patterson Report March, 1972, George Patterson, Sydney.

Pipher, M. 1996, *Reviving Ophelia*, Doubleday, Sydney.

PIECES 1993, *Arena*, September, p. 5.

Povich, M. & Gross, K. 1991, *Current Affairs: a Life on the Edge*, G. P. Putnam's Sons, New York; cited in M. Ehrlich, 1994, 'The Journalism of Outrageousness: Tabloid Television Vs. Investigative News', paper presented to the International Communications Association conference, Sydney, 1994.

Pringle, R. 1981 'The Dialectics of Porn', *Scarlet Woman*, no. 12, March, pp. 3–10.

Raymond, J. 1993, 'Pornography and the Politics of Lesbianism', *Pornography: Women, Violence and Civil Liberties: a Radical New View*, ed. C. Itzin, Oxford University Press, Oxford.

Roiphe, K. 1993, *The Morning After: Sex, Fear and Feminism on Campus*, Little, Brown, New York.

Rosen, J. 1992 'Politics, Vision and the Press: Toward a Public Agenda for Journalism', *The New News v. The Old News: the Press and Politics in the 1990s*, Twentieth Century Fund, New York.

RuPaul 1995, *Lettin' It All Hang Out*, Hyperion, New York.

Scutt, J. 1991, 'The Chilling Effect', *Bulletin*, June 18, pp. 80–82.

—— 1993, 'For Those Who Can Hear', *Australian*, June 4, p. 16.

Sheridan, S. 1993, 'The *Woman's Voice* on sexuality',' *Debutante Nation: Feminism Contests the 1890s*, eds S. Margarey, S. Rowley and S. Sheridan, Allen & Unwin, Sydney.

Snitow, A. 1985, 'Retrenchment Versus Transformation: the Politics of the Antipornography Movement', *Women Against Censorship*, ed. V. Burstyn, Douglas & McIntyre, Vancouver.

Sommers, C. H. 1994, *Who Stole Feminism? How Women Have Betrayed Women*, Simon & Schuster, New York.

Spender, D. 1995, *Nattering on the Net: Women, Power and Cyberspace*, Spinifex, Melbourne.

Strossen, N. 1995, *Defending Pornography: Free Speech, Sex, and the Fight for Women's Rights*, Scribner, New York.

Summers, A. 1994, *Damned Whores and God's Police*, Penguin, Melbourne.

Tasker, J. 1970, 'Censorship in the Theatre', *Australia's Censorship Crisis*, ed. Dutton, G. & Harris, M., Sun Books, Melbourne.

Thompson, J. 1994, 'The Theory of the Public Sphere: A Critical Appraisal', *The Polity Reader in Cultural Theory*, Polity Press, Cambridge.

Turkle, S. 1984, *The Second Self: Computers and the Human Spirit*, Granada, London.

—— 1996, *Life on the Screen: Identity in the Age of the Internet*, Simon & Schuster, New York.

Wacjman, J. 1993, *Feminism Confronts Technology*, Allen & Unwin, Sydney.

Wark, M. 1994, *Virtual Geography*, Indiana University Press, Bloomington and Indianapolis.

—— 1996, 'Internet Porn Censorship', *Australian*, April 4, p. 11.

—— 1994, 'Child's Play', *Columbus' Blindness*, ed. Pybus, C., University of Queensland Press, St Lucia.

Weiss, P. 1989, 'Bad Rap For TV Tabs', *Columbia Journalism Review*, May–June, pp. 24–5.

Wills, S. & Stevens, J. 1980 'Women and Pornography: Sexual Fantasy or Sexual Terrorism', *Scarlet Woman*, no. 11, September, pp. 2–6.

Wollstonecraft, M. 1975, *A Vindication of the Rights of Women*, Penguin, Harmondsworth.

Woolf, N. 1991, *The Beauty Myth*, Vintage, London.

Wright, T. 1996, 'Next Target: Violent Videos', *Sydney Morning Herald*, May 4, p. 1.

'You Can Stop the Flood of Pornography' pamphlet, 1984 Blackfriars Priory, Canberra, ACT.

Zelizer, B. 1991, 'From Home to Public Forum: Media Events and the Public Sphere', *Journal of Film and Video*, vol. 43, no. 1–2.

Index

DEFYING GRAVITY

Dennis Altman

The remarkable life of one of Australia's leading political and social commentators. From growing up gay in Tasmania in the 1950s, to the bathhouses and parties of San Francisco and New York in the 1960s, and his more recent travels in Asia in the 1990s, Dennis Altman's life has taken him on an amazing journey which in many ways mirrors Australia's recent history—its reorientation away from Europe towards Asia and its growing confidence as it moves towards a new century and the Republic.

Born in 1943, Dennis Altman is one of Australia's leading political and social commentators. He studied at Cornell University in the 1960s, and has lectured in politics at Monash, Sydney and now La Trobe universities. His first book, *Homosexual*, was published in 1971 and there have been many since then—including *Power and Community: Organisational and Cultural Responses to AIDS*, his first novel *The Comfort of Men* and a book on the politics of stamps (1993).

DIY FEMINISM

Edited by Kathy Bail

Feminism is not a dirty word for twentysomething women; it offers an outlook that is part of an overall do-it-yourself strategy.

Recently characterised in the media by an older generation of feminists as an often puritanical, narrow-minded generation, this collection shows that young women are in fact streetsmart, engaged and in-ya-face. Here a diverse group of riot grrrls, lipstick lesbians, femocrats, musicians, writers, artists and comedians interpret feminism broadly and confidently, with direct reference to their own experiences. Taking feminist social and political outlooks in their stride, their 1990s survival strategies use everything from a wicked sense of humour to a detailed knowledge of the legal system.

Contributors include: Lisbeth Gorr, Rosie Cross, Natasha Stott Despoja, Rebecca Cox, VNS Matrix, Fotini Epanomitis, Ashley Hay, Cathy Wilcox, Purr and Kaz Cooke.

Kathy Bail is a Sydney-based journalist who has worked as deputy editor of *Cinema Papers* and as a senior writer at *The Independent*. She is now the editor of *Rolling Stone* magazine.

POSTCARDS FROM THE NET

Jon Casimir

Want to find the Spot—not the G one, but THE one? Or find Mr Puddy's homesite? Or the home of the Undead? Or would you rather search out porn (be warned—going to the newsagent's will be much quicker)? More to the point, would you like to be told not just How to use the Net but Why you should and Where you can go?

In this zappy, up-to-the-minute guide, intrepid Net traveller Jon Casimir reports back from the sites he finds and explores the issues—some serious, some not—raised by the explosion in Net culture.

Postcards from the Net is not nerdy or bogged down in Net lingo, and you won't have to be eighteen or under to read it. It is written from an Australian perspective for an Australian audience—rather than assuming we are all, already, part of one big global family. An ambient mix of the discursive and resourceful, this book is the perfect guide for those who have just begun to think about taking the trip into cyberspace, as well as an invaluable resource tool and inspiration for those already out there 'surfing'.

Jon Casimir writes on popular culture and technology for the *Sydney Morning Herald*. He has been published in most major Australian newspapers and magazines and is a regular Mr Rent-an-Opinion on ABC Radio.

JAPAN SWINGS

Politics, culture and sex in the new Japan

Richard McGregor

Centuries of tradition meets pop culture, militarism meets the peace movement, democracy meets autocracy, feminism meets office ladies, and the cautious Japanese bureaucrat meets the cowboy entrepreneur. In the 1990s, Japan has swung from being an unstoppable economic colossus to an economy on the brink of collapse, taking with it the myths and cultural certitudes the West has built up about the country—and that Japan has built up about itself. In the face of such disasters as the Kobe earthquake, the cult of Supreme Truth, and the wild fluctuations on the stockmarket, Japan is now a nation in transition: economically, politically and culturally.

Richard McGregor lived in Tokyo during the most dramatic period in Japan's postwar history and observes the Japanese not through faceless corporations, but with stories of elite mandarins, scheming politicians, ultra-nationalist thugs, and the new generation of young men and women who are transforming the workplace, and the bedroom.

Richard McGregor was until recently Tokyo correspondent for the *Australian* and the ABC. He is now China correspondent for the *Australian*, and is based in Hong Kong.

SEX IN PUBLIC

Australian sexual cultures

Edited by Jill Julius Matthews

In the late 1960s, sex went public. Sex was talked about openly for the first time, sex became organised and went on marches, and feminism and gay liberation were born. Now that the heady days of the sexual revolution are over, what has happened to Australian sexual cultures?

Sex in Public takes us along the highways and byways of sexuality in the 1990s, from lipstick lesbians to cybersex. It explores the fluidity of sexual pleasure, the variety of sexual expressions and sexual communities.

If you thought sex in the 1990s was straightjacketed by AIDS, think again!

Jill Julius Matthews is Director of the Centre for Women's Studies at The Australian National University.

VOLATILE BODIES

Toward a corporeal feminism

Elizabeth Grosz

Volatile Bodies is based on a risky wager: that all the effects of subjectivity, psychological depth and inferiority can be refigured in terms of bodies and surfaces. It uses, transforms and subverts the work of a number of distinguished male theorists of the body (Freud, Lacan, Merleau-Ponty, Schilder, Nietzsche, Foucault, Lingis and Deleuze) who, while freeing the body from its subordination to the mind, are nonetheless unable to accommodate the specificities of women's bodies.

Volatile Bodies explores various dissonances in thinking about the relationship between mind and body. It investigates issues that resist reduction to these binary terms—psychosis, hypochondria, neurological disturbances, perversions and sexual deviation—and most particularly in the enigmatic status of body fluids, and the female body.

Elizabeth Grosz is one of Australia's best-known feminist theorists. She is the author of *Sexual Subversions: Three French feminists* and *Jaques Lacan: A feminist introduction*, and editor of six collections on feminist theory.

DATE DUE